THE PALESTINIAN IMPASSE IN LEBANON

Studies in Peace Politics in the Middle East

1. *The Palestinian Refugees: Old Problems – New Solutions*
   Edited by Joseph Ginat and Edward J. Perkins

2. *The Middle East Peace Process: Vision versus Reality*
   Edited by Joseph Ginat, Edward J. Perkins, and Edwin G. Corr

3. *The Israeli–Palestinian Peace Process: Oslo and the Lessons of Failure – Perspectives, Predicaments and Prospects*
   Edited by Robert L. Rothstein, Moshe Ma'oz and Khalil Shikaki

4. *Water in the Jordan Valley: Technical Solutions and Regional Cooperation*

5. *The Palestinian Impasse in Lebanon: The Politics of Refugee Integration*
   Simon Haddad

Volumes 1 and 2 are published in association with the University of Oklahoma Press

The Palestinian Impasse in Lebanon

The Politics of Refugee Integration

SIMON HADDAD
Foreword by Hilal Khashan

sussex
ACADEMIC
PRESS
BRIGHTON • PORTLAND

Copyright © Simon Haddad 2003

The right of Simon Haddad to be identified as author of this work has been asserted in accordance with the Copyright, Designs and Patents Act 1988.

2 4 6 8 10 9 7 5 3 1

First published 2003 in Great Britain by
SUSSEX ACADEMIC PRESS
PO Box 2950
Brighton BN2 5SP

and in the United States of America by
SUSSEX ACADEMIC PRESS
920 NE 58th Ave Suite 300
Portland, Oregon 97213-3786

All rights reserved. Except for the quotation of short passages for the purposes of criticism and review, no part of this publication may be reproduced, stored in a retrieval system, or transmitted, in any form or by any means, electronic, mechanical, photocopying, recording or otherwise, without the prior permission of the publisher.

British Library Cataloguing in Publication Data
A CIP catalogue record for this book is available from the British Library.

Library of Congress Cataloging-in-Publication Data
Haddad, Simon.
The Palestinian impasse in Lebanon : the politics of refugee integration / Simon Haddad.
p. cm. — (Studies in peace politics in the Middle East ; 4)
Includes bibliographical references and index.
ISBN 1-903900-46-8
1. Refugees, Palestinian Arab—Lebanon. 2. Refugees, Palestinian Arab—Lebanon—Case studies. 3. Lebanon—Politics and government—1990– I. Title. II. Series.
HV640.5.P36H333 2003
956.04—dc21
2003004319

Typeset and designed by G&G Editorial, Brighton
Printed by TJ International, Padstow, Cornwall
This book is printed on acid-free paper.

Contents

Foreword by Hilal Khashan, American University of Beirut	vi
Preface and Acknowledgments	viii
Introduction: Lebanon's Confessional Structure and Palestinian Presence	1

Part I *The Refugees, Lebanon and the Arab–Israeli Conflict*

1	Regional Actors and Peace with Israel	15
2	Integration, Repatriation or Resettlement?	22
3	The Palestinian Factor in the Lebanese Conflict	29
4	Obstacles to Integration and Resettlement	40

Part II *Methodological Criteria: Studying Immigration, Discrimination and Integration*

5	Measuring Attitudes toward Immigration and Immigrants	65
6	The Research Method	75
7	Basic Political Views of Palestinians	82
8	The Socio-Economic Integration of Palestinians	91
9	The Origins and Nature of Popular Attitudes toward Resettlement	103
10	Lebanese Perceptions of Palestinians	118
11	Palestinian Refugees' Socio-Political Attitudes in Lebanon	128

Conclusion: Toward a National Consensus?	141
Questionnaires	
Appendix A: Palestinian Resettlement	149
Appendix B: Palestinian Residents in Lebanese Camps	157
Select Bibliography	162
Index	171

Foreword by Hilal Khashan

The establishment of the Jewish state in 1948 created the Palestinian refugee question – probably the most contentious issue of displacement in modern times. Forming the crux of the Arab–Israeli conflict, most Palestinian refugees dispersed in neighboring Arab countries such as Jordan, Syria and Lebanon. United Nations resolutions demanding the repatriation or compensation of Palestinian refugees, such as UN Resolution 194 (1949), went unheeded by Israel, which continues to enjoy steady and unconditional American support. A series of Arab–Israeli wars led, especially after the 1973 October War, to a march toward peace. Egypt set the stage by signing the Camp David agreement with Israel in 1979; and Jordan followed in its footsteps, concluding its own peace agreement with Israel in 1994. Nevertheless, the Declaration of Principles for Peace between Israel and the PLO, signed on September 13, 1993, under the auspices of then US President Bill Clinton, did not lead to the resolution of the Palestinian critical component, with its refugee core, of the Arab–Israeli conflict.

The stalemated refugee problem did not deter Palestinians from trying to reassemble their lives. The government in Damascus immediately integrated Palestinian refugees who fled to Syria, extending to them comprehensive civil rights. In Jordan, especially after the late King Abdullah I merged the West Bank with Transjordan to form the Hashemite Kingdom of Jordan, Palestinians there received citizenship and predominated the nascent Kingdom's civil and economic sectors. Saudi Arabia's royals naturalized Palestinians settling there, and further Palestinians emigrated to Kuwait. There, they developed the tiny oil-rich state and became a prime example of Palestinian success in the diaspora.

In Lebanon, Palestinian refugees received, on arrival, a lukewarm welcome from the country's confessional elite who saw them as a menace to the fragile political system they ran. They saw to it that Palestinians remained outside Lebanon's political and economic life and doomed them to abysmal poverty. Lebanese authorities treated the refugees harshly and enacted laws that barred them from decent employment. A recent law made it illegal for Palestinians to own, or inherit, real estate. The Lebanese

Foreword by Hilal Khashan

government keeps making it very clear to the world that Palestinian refugees are unwelcome to stay indefinitely on its soil, and never ceases to demand their resettlement outside its territory.

Professor Haddad has embarked on a difficult topic, with which he chooses to deal objectively. He divides his book into two parts; the first part deals with the Palestinian refugees in Lebanon in the context of the country's domestic politics, as well as the broader regional setting. The second part presents the author's empirical findings, which follow a review of refugee-related literature, and an account of his research methodology. His fresh findings and crisp analysis reinforce what we know about Lebanese perceptions about Palestinian refugees living in their country. Hostility toward Palestinians, and blaming them for the country's protracted civil war, reflects the views of the majority of respondents from different sectarian backgrounds, albeit with varying degrees of intensity. Similarly, empathy toward Palestinians was only evident among a minority of respondents.

By and large, the respondents indicated aversion to the permanent resettlement of Palestinians in Lebanon, though they disagreed on the extension of civil rights to the refugees. In a rare manifestation of sectarian affinity, Sunni Muslim respondents appeared more agreeable to entitling Palestinians to basic civil rights than members of other sects. But all in all, the picture does not look promising for the future of a Palestinian presence on Lebanese soil. The majority of respondents, with no regard to sectarian differences, do not approve of permanent resettlement of the refugees, let alone naturalizing them.

This study, which pays attention to Palestinian refugees' perceptions of their conditions in Lebanon, portrays a difficult picture of refugee life. Palestinian respondents included in Haddad's several surveys report pervasive disaffection with their economic situation. One easily senses the aura of despair that characterizes the Palestinian outlook for their future, which they describe as bleak.

Haddad deserves to be commended on his valuable study. He has provided us with an honest and valuable account of how many Lebanese view the presence of Palestinian refugees in their country. He has also opened a window for us to look closely at the silent sufferings of Palestinians in Lebanon. Researchers on the future of Palestinian presence in Lebanon will find Haddad's study pertinent and challenging.

Beirut, March 2003

Preface and Acknowledgements

The fate of Palestinian refugees has drawn widespread political attention in recent years. The prospects for peace between Israel and the PLO generated intensive debate on the future of the refugees, especially since Israel made it clear that it would not allow their repatriation. Political interest in the refugees has not, unfortunately, been matched by academic interest. There remains a serious gap in scholarly writings on Palestinian refugees, particularly in Lebanon. Palestinian refugees in Lebanon present a difficult issue because of the confessional nature of the country's political system. This study seeks to address important questions: How do the Lebanese view Palestinian presence in their country? How do Palestinian refugees perceive their status and future? Is refugee resettlement a workable option for both Lebanese and Palestinians? These questions are recurring themes for all academics, authors and politicians who examine the Palestinian refugee question in Lebanon. Given the particularity and precariousness of the Palestinian presence in the country, several studies have dealt with the subject. Nevertheless, most of these works tend to be descriptive: although there is a wide range of excellent analytic books, the orientation they pursue is generally normative. Another deficiency is the presence of some subjective accounts seeking to offer misinformation in the guise of scholarship.[1]

The present volume seeks to contribute to the existing literature on Palestinian refugees, examining socio-political attitudes related to the status of the sizable Palestinian community residing in Lebanon from a behavioral perspective.

This book examines: (1) the nature and origin of Lebanese socio-political attitudes toward the Palestinian community; (2) their views regarding the prospect of permanent settlement; and (3) major sources and salient manifestations of Palestinian frustration and their amenability to resettlement outside Palestinian territory. This book also seeks to demonstrate

---

[1] For example, Sheikh Farid Elias Al-Khazen's *The Breakdown of The State in Lebanon, 1967–1976* (London: I B.Tauris & Co., 2000) has been criticized for promoting and sensationalizing hate for Arabs and Muslims and for explicit bias.

Preface and Acknowledgements

that for resettlement to be workable in a multi-confessional society that recognizes the primacy of religious communities, the various religious groups need to acquiesce to this alternative; furthermore, the general perceptions among Lebanese of the Palestinian community have to be improved. Unless this occurs, resettlement would threaten the very fabric of Lebanese society and its delicate political structure.

This book is divided into thirteen chapters. An introduction deals with the confessional divisions among the Lebanese people and describes the main characteristics of the country's religious groups, in order to place the Palestinians within the context of Lebanon's political system.

In chapters 1 through 4, a background of the Palestinian refugee crisis in the Middle East is provided and an attempt is made to show the impact of the refugee question on the peace process. The Palestinian role in Lebanese politics is described, as well as the Lebanese authorities' policy toward the refugees from the 1950s until the present.

In chapters 5 and 6, the procedural aspects of the study are laid out on the basis of relevant theoretical contributions and technical considerations that are related to the field work undertaken. Accordingly, a description of the population elements of the study is given, in addition to an account of the process of selecting respondents.

Chapters 7 through 9 are analytical and constitute the core of the book. They deal with the basic political attitudes toward Palestinians and discuss Lebanese views toward their integration and permanent settlement, including Palestinian views on social and political issues pertaining to their status and future.

The study is concluded by assessing the implication of the findings not only on the Arab–Israeli peace process but also on Lebanon's domestic scene, and by voicing recommendations for policymakers.

As with any other scholarly work, this book owes much to external support. The arch of thanks begins with the Notre-Dame University in the person of reverend Boutros Tarabay for his generous contribution to this project. I am profoundly grateful to Professor Hilal Khashan, who first introduced me to social science methodology when I was a graduate student at the American University of Beirut, and who has never failed to provide me with guidance and inspiration. Through his enthusiasm and personal example, he transformed me into a disciple of empirical research.

I am also indebted to my brother Joseph who was particularly cooperative and provided me with all the technical support I needed, and to Mr. Kleo Mitsis who read parts of this book and made valuable stylistic changes. The administration of the questionnaires in the refugee camps would not have been possible without the assistance of Abu Kamal.

I am deeply thankful to my parents, Helen and Ghassan, for their

Preface and Acknowledgements

unfailing support. Finally, I am forever indebted for the steady encouragement and support of my wife Dania and my daughters Rhea and Selena who shared me with my research during the progress of the book.

The Palestinian Impasse in Lebanon

The Politics of Refugee Integration

Introduction
Lebanon's Confessional Structure and Palestinian Presence

The future of the Palestinian refugees has been a core issue in the Arab–Israeli conflict since 1948. Following the initiation of the Middle East peace process in 1991 in Madrid, it has become clear that a satisfactory solution regarding the future of Palestinian refugees residing in Arab host countries is imperative for a durable regional peace. Pending a political solution that determines their fate, more than five million Palestinians continue to be refugees in various Arab countries.

Of all the countries hosting Palestinians, Lebanon confronts probably the most sensitive and serious problems. There is a widespread impression in the country that the future of the Palestinians will be decided by the United States as peace talks reach a decisive stage, and that a large number of refugees will be resettled in Lebanon. Lebanese officials worry, however, that refugee resettlement cannot take place without further eroding the country's precarious demographic composition.

After two decades of civil war, the Palestinian presence has been the subject of much controversial debate – ranging from statements calling for their comprehensive deportation to more careful and pragmatic propositions that they be granted at least some form of civil rights and a more secure form of permanent residence. And while politicians, religious leaders, political parties and scholars have joined the discussion, little attention has been paid to (1) public attitudes *vis-à-vis* the Palestinians as a group, (2) the prospect of their permanent settlement in Lebanon and its expected impact on the country[1] and (3) to Palestinian perceptions of resettlement in and outside of Lebanon.

The claim that foreign plots exist to impose the settlement of Palestinians on Lebanon has been brought forward by the media on several occasions. These reports have increased worries among Lebanese about the probability that Palestinian refugees may stay in the country indefinitely.[2] The issue was especially emphasized in the aftermath of the

Introduction

War of the Camps in 1987. Lebanese media news reported alleged international support for a Palestinian settlement scheme south of Beirut.[3] The debate regarding the fate of Palestinians residing in Lebanon resurfaced with the confirmation in the Oslo Accords of 1993 that an agreement must be put in place to settle the Palestinians in the countries where they currently reside. Moreover, if a solution were reached regarding the Palestinian presence, it would not necessarily provide for their return to their homeland. Not only is the permanent settlement of Palestinians in Lebanon outlawed under Lebanon's constitution, but public statements by Lebanese officials refuse to endorse permanent integration. Lebanese President Emile Lahoud confirmed this policy in 1999 when addressing a conference for Francophone countries in Canada, saying, "All the Lebanese people agree that the permanent settlement of the Palestinian refugees is a time bomb."[4] Other examples of this common political altruism include remarks by Abdullah al-Amin, a prominent Shi'ite Lebanese politician: "The talk about settling the Palestinians does not concern us in any way. We say that the Palestinians must return to Palestine, as we are unable to absorb or settle anyone."[5] Former Education Minister Michel Edde likewise concludes: "Lebanon refuses the implantation of the Palestinians on its territories, since this foreshadows the country's division."[6] Sunni MP Ahmed Karami also expressed his categorical opposition: "While the foreign media has been suggesting that resettlement is going to be imposed on the Lebanese, we think that the Lebanese people, because of their unity and solidarity, can stop any resettlement plan."[7]

Studies, reports and media articles about Palestinian resettlement in Lebanon are numerous, but most of them tend to be descriptive or concerned about the refugees' legal and socio-political standing.[8] Rarely are studies both nationwide and cross-cultural, with a concern for discovering what lies behind social and political relationships. Most importantly there has been little research in which the individual is the unit of analysis; accordingly very few data-based investigations that focus on the link between the social and political orientations of ordinary Lebanese citizens toward Palestinian presence, and Palestinian refugees' perceptions of their situation and status in Lebanon.[9] To these deficiencies may be added the dearth of information about both the relationship between social attitudes held by the Lebanese toward Palestinians and their indefinite settlement in Lebanon – an issue central to national politics and to the Middle East peace process.

In light of the foregoing, it is important to understand how Lebanese citizens look at the Palestinians resident in their country, and especially the prospect that they might settle permanently there. Toward this end, the author conducted a survey exploring several aspects of this question in late

Introduction

1999 and early 2000. Survey questions probed the awareness of issues popular attitudes and expectations.

Equally important is to examine Palestinian camp residents' perceptions of their possible settlement in the country, and also their attitudes to the various solutions to their problem. A secondary survey, conducted in July and August 2002, investigated attitudes related to resettlement related issues inside various Palestinian camps.

The underlying thesis of this study is as follows: (1) In order for Palestinian resettlement to be feasible, there needs to be a general consensus in the country, including acceptance of various aspects and consequences of the extent and circumstances of the resettlement position among the different Lebanese sectarian groups. In a multi-confessional state that recognizes the primacy of religious communities, any decision or policy must satisfy all communities to be workable. (2) There needs also to be a common favorable attitude toward the perceived consequences of resettlement. Accordingly, prior to any resettlement, most Lebanese groups should see such a move as benefiting Lebanese society and in line with their country's national interest and should comply with its occurrence. (3) In order for the resettlement program to work, overall levels of intolerance toward Palestinians need to be low. Minimal social integration and weak inter-communal bonds between Lebanese and Palestinian groups are a major obstacle to achieving resettlement without disrupting peaceful coexistence in the country.

These three elements constitute a conceptualization of "Lebanese attitudes toward resettlement" that is appropriate to the Lebanese context. An essential element to a workable solution is the Palestinian refugees' views regarding their own future in Lebanon, and their opinion toward various proposals to solve their crisis. Whether these match or conflict with those of their Lebanese counterparts can contribute to explaining this complex issue.

The Demographic Make-Up of Lebanon and the Number of Palestinian Refugees

No one knows the exact size of any religious group in Lebanon, although speculative estimates can be made. The principal problem related to determining the population's exact size is that of paucity of statistical data, as no official census has been conducted since 1932. Clearly, due to a number of factors including birthrate and emigration, the old ratio of Christians to non-Christians (6:5) does not hold anymore. On the other hand, a claim that Muslims outnumber Christians by a two-to-one margin[10] is also unlikely to accord with reality.

Introduction

Even official and scholarly references are not in agreement as to the breakdown of Lebanon's population by sect. For example, in 1992, the Interior Ministry estimated the size of the six main religious communities of Lebanon as follows:[11]

Table 0.1 Breakdown of the Lebanese population by religious background (1)

	Total %	Population
Shi'ites	25	1,250,000
Sunnis	23	1,133,000
Druze	6	270,000
Maronites	25	1,250,000
Greek Catholic	6	300,000
Greek Orthodox	10	460,000
Armenian	4	190,000

But Winslow offers a somewhat different assessment:[12]

Table 0.2 Breakdown of the Lebanese population by religious background (2)

	Population	Total %
Shi'ites	1,100,000	30
Sunnis	650,000	18
Druze	210,000	6
Maronites	700,000	20
Greek Catholic	160,000	4
Greek Orthodox	190,000	5

Just as there are no definitive, objective figures concerning the exact numbers of Lebanese from each of the various sects, there are no precise figures for the exact number of Palestinian refugees. Available estimates from contradictory sources, in addition to statistics by the United Nations Relief and Works Agency (UNRWA) – which include only those registered refugees – suggest that the size of the Palestinian community is between 370,000 and 450,000, or 10–12 percent of the country's estimated population. This figure is close to 10 percent of the total number of Palestinians registered by the agency.[13]

Because of Lebanon's complicated social make-up and its delicate sectarian balance, lack of census data is regularly exploited for political purposes – and hence is prone to potential exaggeration. For instance, both the Directorate for Palestinian Refugees Affairs – which was established in the Ministry of Interior to manage Palestinian refugees affairs – and the Lebanese "Surete Generale," or State Security Service, tend to amplify the figures, using them to stress Lebanon's inability to absorb the refugees.

Introduction

Official Palestinian sources also tend to adopt the exaggerated figures to draw attention and seek international support by highlighting the level of their plight.[14]

Moreover, significant demographic shifts have affected Palestinian refugees in Lebanon, including the civil war, the Israeli invasion of 1982 and the 1985–7 "War of the Camps," which resulted in the destruction of several refugee camps and the relocation of many inhabitants to other camps. Such powerful forces dramatically affect Palestinian demographics and attempt to approximate the real size of the community a complicated task.[15]

Lebanon's Confessional Democracy

Before the outbreak of the civil war in 1975, Lebanon was the only Arab state with an enduring democratic experience, compared with other countries in the Middle East. What made its democratic regime unique was its persistence (for more than 30 years until its collapse in 1975) in spite of a multi-confessional society with an overarching Muslim/Christian cleavage and nineteen different sectarian groups. The main element of heterogeneity of Lebanese society is its subdivision among confessional groups, six of which – as noted by tables 1.1 and 1.2 – are of major importance. Three are Muslim (Sunnis, Shi'ites and Druze); three are Christian (Maronites, Greek Orthodox and Greek Catholics).

These groups constitute sets of kinship, religious and communal loyalties to which one belongs by virtue of birth. In fact, so rigid are they – in their static stratification of the Lebanese religious communities, in their substantial endogamy, in their different rank within society, and in the limited social mobility they permit – that some scholars have been prompted to call them outright castes.[16] The importance of the religious community is ably described by Albert Hourani, who concludes that:

> For Muslims and Christians alike consciousness of belonging to a religious community was the basis of political and social obligation; both were conscious of not belonging to the other community; distinctiveness led to suspicion and dislike. The sect persisted as a social entity even after the impulse which gave it birth had died away. To leave one's sect was to leave one's world, and to live without loyalties, the protection of a community, the consciousness of solidarity and the comfort of loyalty.[17]

The term religious community, group, or sect is used to emphasize its social and political functions and significance. It is not so much the religious principles or theological differences (i.e., the actual faiths) that matter; rather, it is the fact that these are religious communities act as social reference groups. Belonging to a religious group limits in a sense, not only one's contact with others but also the kind of occupation open to an individual. Functionally, for the Lebanese, "the religious community is his nation; that is the people to whom he belongs and with whom he identifies".[18] Ghossein adds:[19]

> The sect is a fully-fledged social system characterized by strong internal cohesion, whose members have adopted certain religious tenets voluntarily or by force. This stage of religious behavior has led to a kind of dialectic between religious principles and norms on the one hand, and cultural tenets on the other. One result of this dialectic is that membership in the sect serves mainly as a reference in regard to the world at large. It follows that the different confessional groups always identify themselves in the first place along confessional ties as Maronites, Sunnis, Druze etc. . . . They do not perceive themselves as Lebanese.

Power Sharing and the National Pact

Throughout its modern history, Lebanon has been ruled according to political and territorial arrangements to safeguard the country's sovereignty and autonomy. The most viable of these efforts – because of the multi-confessional nature of Lebanese society – were more the by-product of consent among major communities, discussion and compromise than a result of coercion, force or cruelty. Internal conflict resolution, renewal and reform in Lebanon have been always portrayed in terms of "power sharing" between Muslims and Christians. For any settlement to be workable a compromise was needed; maintaining peaceful coexistence was a function of satisfying the various sectarian groups through the institution of sectarianism or religious denomination.

Since the formation of Greater Lebanon in 1920, the country's main religious groups have been in a constant state of conflict. Conceived under the exclusive angle of religion, the new entity was no more than a forced association of opposed and individualistic communal nations.[20] From its inception, the new state, which comprised what the Maronites consider their social and historical boundaries and character, was marked by deep divisions over its legitimacy. The Maronites feared absorption in the Arab world, and perceived Greater Lebanon as a guarantee for their existence in the midst of Arab Muslim majority. The Muslims, who made up nearly half the population, on the other hand, were against arbitrary incorporation in a Christian-dominated state and sought to strengthen their ties with their Arab environment, even demanding union with Syria. An attempt was made to resolve this divergence in political outlooks with the proclamation of Lebanon's independence in 1943.

Introduction

The National Pact established a fragile balance between Lebanese groups. This compromise solution for the Lebanese communities who were divided in their conception of the republic stipulated that the country's Christians would forego Western protection and ties; meanwhile Muslims agreed to set aside any pan-Arab desires and accept Lebanon's existing geographic boundaries. The pact was built on sectarian representation and attempted to promote stability through accommodation, cooperation and representation.

Pact-makers incorporated into the political system a confessional schism, allocating public offices among confessional groups according to demographic and political weight. The distribution of power in favor of the Christians, which probably did not reflect the demographic realities, even in 1930s and '40s, was a concession by Muslim leaders. The latter wanted "to keep the minds of Christians at rest" and to allay their "minoritarian fears of engulfment by the overall regional Muslim majority." In effect, the pact provided that the Muslim leaders would cease seeking to incorporate Lebanon in a single Arab or Syrian state; instead, they would "consent to the continued existence of Lebanon as an independent and sovereign state in the Arab world." In return the Maronites would cease looking to the West (France) for protection.

The political distribution of power as determined by the National Pact and in accordance with the 1932 census remained a permanent feature of the Lebanese polity despite the apparent demographic changes in the country after 1943. As far as the Maronites were concerned, their demographic status declined, for their population grew at a much slower pace than the Muslims, due to higher Christian emigration and a higher birthrate among Muslims. As Kamal Salibi remarks, "hardly anyone doubted that the balance of numbers in the country had long been tipping increasingly in favor of the Muslims." Despite the fact that Lebanon needed another census for purposes of political, social and economic planning, this survey was not allowed to take place. The idea of taking a new and fair census would obviously have been a political benefit to the Muslims – for it would give them a greater share in power. This was unacceptable to the Christians in power, even if it were to be a census for reform and development planning, and not one that classified the population by religion and sect. Salibi contends: "Any form of census, it was feared, could indirectly reveal demographic facts that were not in the Christian interest."[21]

In fact, until 1975, Christian resistance fiercely and successfully countered Muslim calls for the adjustment of the proportional representation of power.[22] These demands were rejected because, in the eye of the Maronite leadership, they would endanger Maronite political domination and hence the Maronite project of sustaining a Christian democratic heartland in the core of a threatening Arab world.[23]

Within three decades, Christians were asked to give concessions to Muslim demands for greater participation in political power commensurate with their increased demographic weight.[24] Muslim calls for the adjustment in proportional representation were countered by fierce Maronite reaction claiming that "a leading Maronite role is the only guarantee to preserve the security of the community."[25] Maronite domination of key political and military positions was seen as an important guarantee against pan-Arab nationalism and served to calm Maronite worries concerning the country's independence. This eventually led to civil strife in 1958, demonstrating the feebleness of the internal equilibrium and further deepening Christian–Muslim cleavages.

In the 1960s, the resurgence of Arab nationalism and repercussions of the Arab–Israeli conflict further challenged the pact. Expedited by a massive Palestinian military build-up in the country, Lebanon's religious, social, economic and ideological tensions ultimately exploded in a protracted civil war (1975–90). This war was fought over a number of issues, including the balance of power in government, the role of the armed Palestinian groups, the redistribution of wealth, and Lebanon's foreign policy orientation. The conflicting attitudes held by Christians and Muslims over the Palestinian presence in the country revealed the precariousness of the Lebanese political system and the degree to which the Lebanese were not genuinely integrated.

The Ta'if Accord

Of all the peace initiatives to solve the Lebanese crisis, only the Document of National Understanding, known as the Ta'if Accord, signed by Lebanese MPs in 1989 under Arab sponsorship, succeeded in ending the civil war and in establishing conditions for peace. The Ta'if Accord not only attempted to achieve inter-communal equilibrium but, like the 1943 National Pact, embraced a consensual, sectarian logic and dictated procedures to distribute public offices among the various communities.[26] Although not all parties consented to the accord, its imposition as a solution in the form of a communal contract was made possible because no party or community emerged victorious during the war and also because no community could claim a majority in terms of demographic weight. Maintaining the peace, therefore, was – and still is – a matter of maintaining a balance of sharing power and of preserving the rights of communities that view themselves as the bedrock upon which the state of Lebanon is constructed.

The Ta'if Accord brought basic modifications concerning the sharing and allocation of political power but did not alter the fundamental char-

Introduction

acter of the first republic of 1943. The principle of sectarian proportionality remained, but the proportion of Muslims to Christians in the legislature increased to 50:50 instead of 6 to 5. Though Lebanon still has a Christian president, his authority no longer towers over the Sunni prime minister or the Shi'ite speaker of Parliament.

The agreement also wrought a change in the political structure to take account of the new power balances among the communities: the decline of the Maronites and the growth of the Sunnis and the Shi'ites. In post-Ta'if Lebanon, the Christians argue, with great bitterness, a biased interpretation of the accord has been arbitrarily imposed on them. This agreement was essentially meant to end the political stalemate in the country and reconcile the Lebanese around a program of internal reforms. Although, the accord ended sectarian violence in Lebanon, it nevertheless failed to promote cooperation among Lebanese groups.

Political divisions in Lebanon are intense. The political nature of the Lebanese system and the difficulty in achieving national understanding over the future of the country is complex. The Palestinians are treated as if they were threatening to become Lebanon's legitimate twentieth sect.

Notes

1. In addition to increased attention to the Palestinian refugee question in Lebanon, a conference on Palestinian resettlement was held in 1999, "Lebanese Identity: Between Naturalization and Implantation," at the University of Saint Esprit, Kaslik, on November 11 and an academic workshop entitled "Opposing Resettlement" at the University of Saint Joseph, organized by the Research Center for Arab Law, Beirut on November 26, 1999. These events grouped prominent Lebanese figures, and even the prime minister. This trend received additional support with the announcement that Lebanese clerics of all sects intended to hold the conference to take a harsh stance on the matter on July 29.
2. See for instance the Lebanese weekly *Al-Hawadeth* (1166) (March 9, 1979), pp. 53–5.
3. See Khalil Abu Antoun "Hal Yatawatan Al Filistiniyyun Bayn Alawali Wa Sinyq?" (Are The Palestinians Going to Be Resettled Between Al-Awali and Sinyq?), *An-Nahar Al-Arabi Wa Al Duwali* (546), (October 1987), pp. 15, 19–25 and "Tawtin al Filistinyyin fi Iqlim Al Tuffah" (Palestinian Permanent Settlement in Iqlim Al Tuffah), (585), (July 25–31, 1988), pp. 8–9.
4. Nicholas Blanford, "No Early Solution in Sight," *The Middle East* (November 1999), p. 18.
5. N. Abd-al-Samad, "Palestinian Settlement in Lebanon," *Al-Majallah* (April 9–15, 1995).
6. *Al-Nahar*, Beirut, November 26, 1999.
7. *Al-Nahar*, July 29, 1999.
8. Nawaf Salam, "Between Repatriation and Resettlement: Palestinian refugees

Introduction

in Lebanon," *The Journal of Palestine Studies*, Autumn 24 (1) (1994); Rosemary Sayyigh, *Too Many Enemies: The Palestinian experience in Lebanon* (London and New Jersey: Zed Books Ltd, 1994); Farid al-Khazen "Permanent Settlement of Palestinians in Lebanon: A recipe for conflict," *Journal of Refugee Studies*, 10 (3) (1997); Donna Arzt, *Refugees into Citizens: Palestinians and the end of the Arab–Israeli conflict* (Council on Foreign Relations Press, 1996); Susan M. Akram, "Palestinian Refugees and Their Legal Status: Rights, politics and implications for a just solution," *Journal of Palestine Studies* 31 (3) (2002), pp. 36–51.

9 Hilal Khashan, "Palestinian Resettlement in Lebanon: Behind the debate," *Montreal Studies on the Contemporary Arab World* April (1994); Simon Haddad, "The Palestinian Predicament in Lebanon," *Middle East Quarterly* 7 (1) (2000), pp. 29–40.

10 Charles Winslow, *Lebanon: War and politics in a fragmented society* (London and New York: Routledge, 1996), p. 303.

11 Gérard Figuie, *Le point sur le Liban* (Beyrouth: Anthologie, 1996), p. 39.

12 Charles Winslow, *Lebanon*, p. 303.

13 See "Palestinians in Lebanon: Report on the Conference Held at Oxford, September 27–30," (Oxford: Center for Lebanese Studies, 1996), p. 10. More recently – during a conference entitled "Lebanese Identity: Between Naturalization and Implantation," attended by the author on Palestinian Resettlement at the University of Saint Esprit, Kaslik, Lebanon, on November 26, 1999 – Maronite deputy Naamatullah Abi-Nasr, former president of the Maronite League, offered a figure of 12 percent. This is compared to other Arab host countries where Palestinian represent 1 percent of the population in the United Arab Emirates for example, and only 0.1 percent in Egypt and in Saudi Arabia. Also, see Fafo: "Living Conditions of Palestinian Refugees in camps and Gatherings in Lebanon," February 1999.

14 See PRCS: Medical Services, Past, Present, and Future in Lebanon (Beirut: Palestine Red Crescent Society, 1992), p.38, as quoted in Rosemary Sayigh "The Palestinians in Lebanon: A painful present and uncertain future," *Majallat al-Dirasat al-Filastiniyya* 13 (Winter 1993), p. 16.

15 Hala Nawfal Rizkallah, *Al-Falastiniiuun fi lubnan wa suria dirasat dimougrafiat moukaranat* (The Palestinians in Lebanon and Syria: A comparative demographic study), (Beirut: Dar Al-Jadid, 1998).

16 S. A Saade, *The Social Structure of Lebanon: Democracy or servitude?* (Beirut: Edition Dan An-Nahar, 1993), pp. 10–11

17 Albert Hourani, *Syria and Lebanon* (London: Oxford University Press, 1954), pp .63–4.

18 R. E. Crow, "Electoral Issues: Lebanon", in J. M. Landau, F. Ozbudun and F. Tachau (eds.), *Electoral Politics in The Middle East: Issues, voters and elites* (London: Croom Helm, 1980), pp. 153–87.

19 A. Ghossein, "Geography in the study of the Lebanese structure and crisis," *Haliyyat*, 25 (1982) pp. 23–45.

20 Edmond Rabath, *La Formation Historique Du Liban Politique et Constitutioneelle* (The Formation of Historical and Political Lebanon), (Beirut: Publications de L'Universite Libanaise 1973), p. 128.

Introduction

21 Cited in Edmond Melhem, "Workings and Shortcomings of the Lebanese Political System," *Middle East Quarterly* 3 (10) (1996).
22 Hence, in order to defend their political interests, the Maronites refused to allow another census, and insisted that the most powerful political position – the presidency – be kept for them.
23 Maronite domination of key political and military positions was seen as an important guarantee against pan-Arab nationalism and served to calm their worries concerning the country's independence. Pro-West vs. Pro-Arab orientations continued to divide the Lebanese.
24 Hani Faris, "The Failure of Peacemaking in Lebanon: 1975–1989," in Deidre Collings (ed.), *Peace for Lebanon? From war to reconstruction* (Boulder, CO: Lynne Rienner Publishers, 1994), pp. 18–30.
25 Mahmood Ayoub, "Lebanon between Religious Faith and Political Ideology," in Deidre Collings (ed.), *Peace for Lebanon? From war to reconstruction* (Boulder, CO: Lynne Rienner Publishers, 1994), pp. 241–48.
26 Joseph Maila, "The Ta'if Accord: An Evaluation," in Deidre Colling (ed.), *Peace for Lebanon? From war to reconstruction* (Boulder, CO: Lynne Rienner Publishers, 1994), pp. 31–44.

Part I

The Refugees, Lebanon and the Arab–Israeli Conflict

1
Regional Actors and Peace with Israel

This chapter explains Lebanese–Syrian strategy in pursuing peace talks in view of Lebanon's military and political disadvantage *vis-à-vis* Israel. It describes Lebanon's pressing problems, most notably the refugee issue.

Lebanon, Syria and the Peace Process

Lebanon's civil war came to an end in the autumn of 1990 when, with tacit approval from Washington, Syrian forces crushed the rebellion of General Michel Aoun, who had resisted implementing the Ta'if Accord of 1989. This agreement, aimed at ending the war and regulating the Lebanese political system, was signed by Lebanese MPs at a conference in Ta'if, Saudi Arabia. The accord set out steps to impose the central government's sovereignty throughout all of Lebanon. Unfortunately, more than 13 years after the signing, Lebanon is still wracked by problems and continues to be an arena of confrontation of the ongoing Arab–Israeli conflict.

Moreover, Syria's influence on Lebanon has grown tremendously since the late 1980s. An intricate system of Syrian control – combining military and intelligence ubiquitousness, economic penetration, a sizable Syrian civilian presence, control of the Lebanese military command, and meticulous screening of domestic office aspirants in an essentially patronage system, where political appointments and personal loyalties appear to coincide – has ensured official Lebanese compliance with Syrian guidelines.[1] Few political decisions are made without consulting Damascus, and it is widely understood that Syria routinely intervenes in all affairs of the Lebanese government. Local decisions are tailored to suit Syrian preferences, and no decision is made that will have even the remote likelihood of offending Damascus.

Thus, since 1991 Syria has apprehended Lebanon politically and diplomatically. A network of agreements and pacts even tie the two countries closer together, serving to legitimize Syrian meddling in Lebanese affairs. These range from the 1991 Treaty of Brotherhood, Cooperation and Coordination, to a pact on defense and security, signed the same year – in addition to several bilateral agreements regulating agriculture, social and economic affairs, health and the movement of individuals and goods. The common denominator is that each agreement has served to bring Lebanon further under Syria's wing.

In February 1993, early in his tenure as Lebanese Prime Minister, Rafik Hariri outlined some parameters for negotiations with Israel: "Lebanon is willing to sign any agreement with Israel, short of a peace treaty, based on United Nations Security Council Resolution 425" (the 1978 resolution that calls for the withdrawal of Israeli forces from Lebanon). Hariri rejected any association with Resolutions 242 and 338, which deal with the Arab–Israeli conflict and the principle of land-for-peace, since the occupation of southern Lebanon by Israel is unequivocally rejected in Resolution 425, and where, unlike 242 and 338, there is no suggestion of a principle of territorial adjustment. Hariri also announced his refusal to wait for progress by other parties negotiating with Israel.

Thanks to Syria's tight grip over the country, Hariri's "independent" position did not last long; and by October 1993, Lebanon announced a policy of total coordination with its "big brother." Even today, Lebanese officials still unanimously echo the Syrian stance on the symbiosis of the two countries' peace tracks with Israel. They also vividly remember another "independent" attempt – former Lebanese President Amin Gemayel's infamous botched program to seek a separate peace treaty with Israel, often referred to as the May 17, 1983 Agreement. Syria's punitive response at the time was to curtail the Lebanese government's authority in most regions. Thus, in view of the demise of the May 17 Agreement, it is probably safe to assert that Lebanon cannot conclude a peace agreement with Israel without Syrian overlordship.[2]

The Role of the United States

Diplomatically, Lebanon has been relatively isolated on the international level since 1993, when it became clear that Beirut had tied its fate to Damascus, a position reluctantly recognized by the United States. And while the US has continued to emphasize its continuing commitment to the country's territorial integrity, to the withdrawal of all foreign forces from Lebanese soil, and to the re-establishment of peace and security, US policy in the region under President Bill Clinton was remarkably partial to Israeli perspectives, and especially so in southern Lebanon, where Washington often offered unconditional support for Israel's actions. As such,

Washington tolerated Israel's refusal to relinquish a "buffer zone" of Lebanese territory along the border, captured in 1978 – with Tel Aviv insisting the land was necessary to prevent anyone from using southern Lebanon to launch possible attacks against northern Israel.

This penchant for US restraint was perhaps most clearly demonstrated in April 1996, during Israel's "Grapes of Wrath" operation, when more than a hundred civilians were killed by Israeli shelling of a UN compound in Qana. Despite strong evidence to the contrary, Israel claimed that it did not know there were refugees in the building, that the site was not even a direct target, and that it had been firing at Hizbullah targets which were, in fact, hundreds of meters away. It then cited a "cartographic error" for the mistake. Moreover, although Israel's presence in southern Lebanon clearly violated UN Resolution 425, which the United States had sponsored, Clinton accepted Israel's assertions that it was acting only to protect its own security. He took no further action except to emphasize Washington's support for Israel.

Many Lebanese complain that the United States does not seem to take their country's role in the peace process seriously, yet it expects them to assume an independent political line from that of Syria. When former Secretary of State Madeleine Albright stopped briefly in Beirut during a Middle East peace trip in September 1999, she antagonized the Lebanese by taking Palestinian resettlement for granted and demanding immediate cessation to all Hizbullah military operations in order to create an atmosphere favorable to the peace talks.

Syrian Negotiating Strategy

The absence of a well-articulated US policy on Lebanon – beyond general declarations of good intent – has served to isolate Lebanon and has arguably further pushed it into Syria's "brotherly" embrace. This has become clearly understood by Israeli officials, who eventually pulled back their troops unilaterally from southern Lebanon in May 2000. That move was meant to deprive Syria of an important bargaining chip in negotiations with Israel. For the Syrians, Israel's withdrawal was interpreted as an indication of success. For Syrian President Bashar Asad, Lebanon will remain important for Syria's security, and he has no plans to abdicate Syrian influence there as part of a settlement with Israel.

In fact, it is the "special" relationship between Damascus and Hizbullah that makes the former's position in Lebanon so overwhelming and continues to encourage American acquiescence to Syrian overlordship in Lebanon. Syria has helped Hizbullah become the eminent military force in Lebanon, wherein it refuses to submit even to the national army. Syria has also placed Hizbullah sympathizers in key army positions, thus forestalling the possibility that the latter might turn against the former.[3] The end good of Syria's Hizbullah policy is that it "convinces" the US and Israel that the fate of this group, much-maligned to both, lies squarely in the hands of Damascus; hence, the need to treat Syria as a regional power.

The Hizbullah card also plays well into the hands of Syria by making a case for maintaining her military presence in Lebanon. As an extension of Syrian policy, Hizbullah continues to target Israeli objectives under the pretext that when Israel withdrew from south Lebanon in May 2000, it left many unresolved issues in the border area between Israel, Lebanon and Syria. In reality, when Israel pulled out of Lebanon, it withdrew almost entirely, keeping just the tiny Shebaa Farms area. This small piece of land – which helps protect the Golan Heights and which Israel took from Syria in 1967 but has promised to return,[4] – has been at the center of controversy: Syria says that the territory is in fact Lebanese, and hence maintains that the Israeli withdrawal has not been completed. However, on several occasions, Israeli warplanes have also attacked Syrian military positions in Lebanon in retaliation for Hizbullah operations. Since these attacks, the limited conflict in the Shebaa Farms now has the potential to explode into an unwanted war between Syria and Israel, and the specter of the Israeli–Palestinian conflict becoming a regional one has again been raised.

Equally, Syria has no intention of allowing the Lebanese Army to assume any real authority in southern Lebanon and along the international border. This way, it can maintain another front, or theater of operations, from which it can harass or attack Israel. Syrian strategy is thereby promoted: Lebanese authorities are forced to acquiesce to an unabated Palestinian armed presence. Lebanon contains substantial Palestinian refugee camps whose members are anxious to become involved in the Intifada, or uprising against Israeli occupation. The Lebanese government has for the most part prevented them from directly participating, but that could end. Syria could also provide more support for Hizbullah to widen its area of operations.

In an explicit form of opposition to Syrian policy, the Lebanese authorities insisted that Islamic Jihad terminate its military operations in southern Lebanon. In October and early November 1999, this anti-Israeli Palestinian movement announced that it had begun attacks against Israel in collaboration with Hizbullah. The Lebanese government responded, albeit without resorting to military action, by persuading Jihad to withdraw its fighters from southern Lebanon. Nevertheless, Palestinian Jihad representatives in Lebanon declared, with tacit Syrian approval in order to send signals to the Israelis, that they were ready to conduct cross-border raids following Israel's May withdrawal.

Regional Actors and Peace with Israel

Despite Syria's hegemonic position in Lebanon, some politicians were still able to advocate crucial Lebanese concerns, which appear to solicit extensive public support, primarily among members of Lebanon's Christian community. In 1995, Simon Karam, the former Lebanese ambassador in Washington, conveyed to the public the gist of private discussions among the local, political and economic circles on what they want for their country from peace with the Jewish state. The Lebanese insist that the internal balance of their country – which has been tipped due to Syrian meddling in the country's domestic and foreign affairs – is restored to enable its competent business class to assume a vital role in the growing Middle Eastern economy, one commensurate with its capabilities.[5] Apart from economics, the Lebanese expected (1) full Israeli withdrawal from Lebanese territory; (2) the consolidation of Lebanese independence by extending their sovereignty over the entire country – an allusion to Syria's control of most of it; (3) the release by Israel of 151 detainees; (4) the recovery of two key water sources, the Wazzani Springs and the Hasbani River, each an important tributary to the Jordan River; and (5) public opposition to the permanent settlement of Palestinian refugees in Lebanon.

As soon as Israel withdrew its troops from the south, Lebanese leaders began to re-examine their agenda by voicing demands, each of which, of course, enhanced the Syrian negotiating position. Among these were that the Lebanese Army not be deployed in the occupied area, a decision linked to Lebanese–Syrian coordination which refuses to grant Israel any security guarantees concerning its northern border.[6]

But leaders also added new items to their agenda. Prior to the Israeli withdrawal, in December 1999, Prime Minister Salim Hoss announced that seven villages on the other side of the 1949 UN demarcation line between Israel and Lebanon rightfully belonged to Lebanon and that their recovery remained "a Lebanese demand."[7] Thus, as Israel's preparations for a pullout continued unabated throughout the spring of 2000, the Syrians realized that a more viable pretext for the continuation of paramilitary attacks was now needed to discourage an Israeli withdrawal. The aforementioned Shebaa Farms,[8] a territorial claim which had never before even been mentioned by a representative of the Lebanese government, was now brought to the fore.

Lebanese scholars such as Ghassan Salameh (who in 2000 became culture minister) concede that the issue of resettling Palestinians, the vast majority of whom are Sunni Muslims, is the most stubborn negotiating item pertaining to the Lebanese track.[9] The current negotiating process, begun in Madrid in 1991, addresses the Palestinian issue in two ways. First, because the matter affects all Arab states hosting Palestinians, one track of multilateral talks is devoted to this issue. Secondly, it was placed on the agenda of the "final status" negotiations between the Palestinian Authority and the Israelis.

What most frightens Lebanon, however, is the likelihood that its own Palestinian population will be neglected in both tracks. Beirut would like the talks to provide for the Palestinians' departure, but doubts that will happen and lacks the leverage to accomplish its goal. Lebanon has no presence in the talks between Israel and Syria that bode to reshape its neighborhood. Lebanon is also absent from the multilateral talks' Refugee Working Group, chaired by Canada, since that group's main objective is to improve the conditions of Palestinian refugees without considering their repatriation – an approach unacceptable to Syria.

Syrian officials have argued that the multilateral talks, which deal with the environment, economic development, security, water, and the issue of refugees, serve to lend legitimacy to Israel, conferring the prizes of peace before Israel has earned them by withdrawing from occupied Arab territory. It also withdrew from the bilateral talks in 1999 between itself and Israel because Israel's then Prime Minister Ehud Barak ruled out the refugees' return to Israel, suggesting instead, "a solution for them should be found in the countries where they are now living."[10]

In view of Israel's position, Beirut refuses to participate in discussing the refugee question unless repatriation is part of the negotiations.

Having examined the basic regional factors that shape Lebanon's position in the peace process, including its attitude toward the refugee issue, it is necessary now to place the question of the Palestinian refugees in its appropriate historical context.

Notes

1   Hilal Khashan and Simon Haddad, "The Coupling of the Syrian–Lebanese Peace Tracks: Beirut's options," *Security Dialogue* 30 (2) (July 2000), pp. 201–14.
2   The linkage between the Syrian and Lebanese tracks has been a constant in the position of Damascus and Beirut as suggested by Prime Minister Rafik Hariri, who ruled out any step by his government to revive stalled Arab–Israeli negotiations, declaring that the Lebanese will never make peace with Israel until the Syrians do. Hariri made it clear that his government will follow where Syria leads, asserting that the differences between Israel and Syria must be addressed first because they "are much more important and much more strategic than the issues that separate Lebanon and Israel." "Neither Syria nor Lebanon will sign a peace treaty with Israel without the other," Hariri said.
3   The Syrian Army units position near the centers of decision-making in Lebanon: the Presidential Palace, the Defense Ministry and other strategic establishments. The extent of Syrian military deployment in Lebanon has angered the Council of Maronite Bishops who, on September 20, 2000, issued

an appeal condemning Syrian trespassing on the "symbols(s) of national unity." The text of the appeal is available at http://www.clao.com/articl19.html.
4   For Lebanon's Prime Minister Rafik Hariri, Israel continues to violate UN Resolution 425 and illegitimately occupy the Shebaa Farms, which Syrian President Bashar Asad reaffirmed was Lebanese territory (*The Daily Star*, Beirut, June 29, 2001).
5   *An-Nahar*, Beirut, July 5, 1995.
6   *The Daily Star*, Beirut, July 6, 2000.
7   However, it soon became clear that Israel was willing to settle for the mere cessation of hostilities. Since the seven villages mentioned above are internationally recognized as Israeli territory, Israeli officials were confident that the Syrians and Lebanese would not try to use this claim to legitimize continued Hizbullah attacks.
8   Israeli forces seized a piece of territory during the 1967 Six Day War called the Shebaa Farms, a 25-square kilometer area consisting of 14 farms located south of Shebaa, a Lebanese village on the western slopes of Mount Hermon.
9   *An-Nahar*, Beirut, June 30, 1995.
10 Amira Hass, "The refugees of peace," *Ha'aretz*, Wednesday, July 21, 1999.

2

Integration, Repatriation or Resettlement?

Since their exodus from Palestine in 1948, the Palestinian refugees in Arab host countries have been confronted with various solutions ranging from full integration in Arab societies to repatriation or resettlement outside their homeland.

Background to the Palestinian Refugee Crisis

The Palestinian refugee crisis accelerated on April 18, 1948 when several thousand Palestinians fled their homes and poured into neighboring Arab countries.[1] As Israeli historian Benny Morris has noted, along with the establishment of the State of Israel, the refugee problem was the major political consequence of the 1948 war and became one of the intractable components of the Arab–Israeli conflict.[2] Palestinians and Israelis approach the question of the refugees and the right of return from radically different perspectives. The Palestinian narrative maintains that the Zionists forcibly expelled the Arab refugees in 1948. The Palestinians insist on the right of the refugees to return to their homes and demand that Israel unilaterally acknowledge its complete moral responsibility for the injustice of the refugees' expulsion. In contrast, the Israeli narrative rejects the refugees' right of return. Israel argues that it was the Arabs who caused the Palestinian refugee problem, by rejecting the creation of the State of Israel and declaring war upon it – a war that, like most wars, created a refugee problem, including a Jewish one.

In the early years after the creation of the Israeli state, many Palestinians hoped that the international community would come to their rescue and restore their national and natural rights. They therefore chose to remain politically and militarily inactive in the diaspora, trusting that the world would support their cause.[3] They fiercely rejected resettlement schemes and preferred to remain refugees than give up claims to their land.[4]

Integration, Repatriation or Resettlement?

Resettlement Schemes and Proposals

During the 1949 Lausanne conference a proposal was put forward that Lebanon might resettle 100,000 Palestine refugees, which was roughly the number then estimated to be destitute there (in the same year). However, the Lebanese delegation did not adopt the suggestion for they recognized that the possibilities of settling refugees in an already thickly populated and intensively cultivated country were very limited. Lebanon already had a population of over 1,127,000, while the whole of the cultivated area was cropped annually, with little land then uncultivated. The rural population in 1944 was estimated to be about 750,000, and was dependent on 1.3 million acres of cultivated land, or 1.5 acres per head.[5] Moreover, even then there was a definite scarcity of land and a tendency for rural people to drift to the towns. A large part of the village population had always supplemented its income by urban work and by remittances from emigrants abroad.

However, in April 1949 the Public Works Ministry prepared a program calling for a substantial increase in the quantity of irrigated lands, the major points of which depended on the utilization of the waters of the Litani River in the south, the Barid River in the north, and Lake Yamuna in the Bekaa Valley. The ministry claimed that if these schemes were fully implemented, twice the amount of land could be irrigated, and much badly needed electric power could be generated. But in fact, these irrigated lands would probably not have provided a livelihood for any besides the rural population. Even those authorities who felt that an additional 745,000 acres, then uncultivated, could be used, and that irrigation schemes could be made to cover 100,000 acres, did not think the Lebanese agricultural economy capable of absorbing substantial numbers of refugees.[6]

Accordingly, the only chance for the permanent settlement of any significant number of refugees into Lebanon would be the economic development of the resources not only of Lebanon but also of the neighboring Syria. This might permit the absorption of refugees with commercial and other urban skills. (Obviously, any significant expansion thus caused in the Lebanese economy would make the need for an expanded agricultural economy, through expanded irrigation, even greater.) Such a development might offer acceptable social and economic conditions to a substantial number of refugees from such cities as Jaffa, Haifa and Acre, whose settlement presented special problems.

At this time, Beirut, the Lebanese capital, was already an important port and commercial center, with a population of some 264,000 (about 22% of the total national population), while the neighboring town of Tripoli had gained from the building by the Iraq Petroleum Company of a second pipe to the city, and from improvements to the refinery there.[7] Syria itself had important towns, the chief being Damascus and Aleppo, and the urban population of Syria accounted for some 30 percent of its total population. If communications could be improved, if existing small-scale industries (e.g., leatherwork of all sorts, textiles, silver inlay and copper work, cement canning and preserving, etc.) could be organized and expanded, and capital and markets assured, it was thought possible that a few thousand craftsmen and townsmen among the refugees could gradually be absorbed into Lebanon.

Lebanon at the time also had a rapidly increasing population and limited resources. But even if the general development of the country were to proceed satisfactorily during the next few years, it was still felt there would probably continue to be considerable opposition to the settlement of refugees, on both economic and religious grounds. The acceptance of refugees was seen as a possible danger to the delicate balance between the country's Christian and Muslim communities. The general conclusion of Lebanese policy-makers was that there was only a very slight possibility that any number of refugees might be absorbed into Lebanon – at least in the years following the creation of the State of Israel.

The Refugees' Right of Return

The most important piece of international legislation on Palestinian refugees is undoubtedly UN Resolution 194 (III) of December 11, 1948 – the essence of which is to guarantee Palestinians the right to return home and to demand compensation: "Refugees wishing to return to their homes and live at peace with their neighbors should be permitted to do so at the earliest practicable date and that for refugees choosing not to return, compensation should be paid by the governments or authorities responsible."[8]

The main outcome of Resolution 194 was the establishment of the Palestine Conciliation Commission, which was entrusted with the task of working out the logistics of the solution. However, since this resolution could not be implemented, UN focus shifted to the humanitarian dimension, in an attempt to improve the conditions of Palestinian refugees in the host countries. For this purpose, the UN Relief and Works Agency (UNRWA) was established by the UN General Assembly on December 8, 1949 as an operational, non-political agency to take responsibility for the humanitarian aspects of the Palestinian refugee problem with a secondary aim to promote conditions of peace and security in the Middle East. It was created to assist Palestinian refugees in the fields of education, work, healthcare and relief. Although the agency's mandate was intended to be temporary, its existence has been perpetuated because of the refugee problem's intractability.

Integration, Repatriation or Resettlement?

Since UNRWA's mandate was based on the Economic Survey Mission reports (late 1949), which specifically recommended the socio-economic integration of the refugees in the host countries through the provision of work opportunities, a large part of the agency's efforts in the early years involved development/resettlement schemes. These ranged from small-scale temporary "relief works" in 1950–1 (such as terracing, reforestation and road construction) to ambitious infrastructure works (such as land reclamation and construction of irrigation systems) in the Sinai and the Jordan Valley from 1952 to 1956.

It was because of the emphasis on resettlement that UNRWA, despite assurances of the humanitarian nature of its efforts, was from the outset seen in Palestinian political circles as having been created by the Western powers to liquidate the refugees' political rights through socio-economic means. Refugee opposition to the resettlement efforts in the early to mid-1950s was such that by the end of the decade, UNRWA was obliged to terminate these programs and reorient its mandate toward general and vocational education.[9]

By the mid-1960s, it was evident that the UN plan had little chance of success as it attempted to solve a political problem using an economic approach, especially as the Arab states were not prepared to cooperate on the large-scale development projects originally foreseen by the agency as a means of alleviating the Palestinians' situation.

The principal known Israeli initiative took place in the summer of 1949. Under pressure from the United States, and in view of Arab refusal (at that year's Lausanne conference) to discuss agreed borders until the refugee issue had been resolved, the Ben-Gurion government agreed to absorb 100,000 refugees into Israel within the framework of a general settlement. This number would have included some 35,000 refugees whose return had already been negotiated and was under way. But Israel's decision was made conditional upon Arab agreement, at Lausanne, to a comprehensive peace, including resettlement of the remaining refugees in Arab countries. Discussion within the Israeli government at the time also touched upon the possibility of absorbing a larger number of refugees, on condition that the Gaza Strip (with some of its refugee population) would be transferred from Egyptian to Israeli control, thereby improving Israel's military security situation *vis-à-vis* Egypt. Ultimately, however, the Arabs rejected the Israeli offer, after which Israel retracted it.

In 1952, the UN Refugee Rehabilitation Fund offered the Arab states $200 million to find homes and jobs for the refugees. The Arab states used some of the money for relief work, but did not apply for the greater part of the fund. The Arab governments were unwilling to contribute to any plan that could be interpreted as encouraging resettlement.[10] They preferred to hang on to their own interpretation of Resolution 194, which they believed

Integration, Repatriation or Resettlement?

would eventually lead to repatriation. The Palestinians' only other hope was that the Arab states would resolve the problem, whether by force or diplomacy.

Palestine was now the pre-eminent Arab concern, and the recovery of Palestine became the principal rallying cry of Arab nationalists. At the same time, Palestine became an internal political issue of great salience, particularly in the pan-Arab core states. Leaders vied with one another in expressing their fidelity to the cause. Authentic as this support undoubtedly was, it remained diffuse and resistant to transformation into effective policy. In the prevailing climate of Arab nationalism of the 1950s and 1960s – with the Arab Socialist Ba'ath Party emerging in Syria and, simultaneously, Gamal Abdel Nasser's rise in Egypt to become the predominant Arab nationalist leader – conciliatory public statements on Arab rights in Palestine became the main legitimizing force for the policies of Arab leaders: "The refugees are the cornerstone in the Arab struggle against Israel. The refugees are the armaments of the Arabs and Arab Nationalism."[11]

Many Palestinians believed in the Arab nationalist ideal and saw the restoration of their homeland taking place within the broader framework of the unification of the Arab world, chiefly under the leadership of Egypt's President Nasser. The latter had himself pledged to sweep away all traces of Zionism, imperialism and the forces of reaction in the Arab world, telling Radio Cairo on June 27, 1961 that: "The refugees will not return while the flag of Israel flies over the soil of Palestine. They will return when the flag of Palestine is hoisted over Arab Palestine."[12]

Thus, the mood in the Arab world was one of defiance toward, and confrontation with, Israel and its Western supporters. Resettlement and reintegration plans for the Palestinian refugees were dismissed as a Zionist and imperialist conspiracy to remove the Palestinian question from the agenda. The official Israeli position, on the other hand, has always been that there can be no return of the refugees to Israeli territories, and that the only solution to the problem was their resettlement in the Arab states or elsewhere. Prime Minister David Ben-Gurion was quoted as saying: "Peace is vital – but not at any price."[13]

Given Israeli refusal to comply with UN Resolution 194 and the Arab states' unwillingness to accept the permanent status quo involving hundreds of thousands of refugees on their soil, the plight of the refugees was to continue and become a local problem for Arab host countries.

The resurgence of Arabism coincided with an increase in Soviet interest in Middle Eastern affairs. This was translated into large-scale military and economic aid to Egypt and Syria, the two Arab countries championing anti-Western policy and slogans at the time. Thus, the Middle East was thrown into the mire of superpower bipolarity, and with it, the trauma of the Palestinian refugees receded to an issue of secondary importance. Officially, the Arabs appeared more concerned with recovering Arab rights in Palestine than with improving the miserable social and economic condition of the refugees, and in consequence they received little attention beyond UNRWA's humanitarian operations.

The 1967 military defeat of the front-line Arab regimes had, among others, two major implications for the Palestinians: First, approximately 360,000 Palestinians were forced to leave the West Bank and Gaza Strip for Jordan, Syria, Lebanon and Egypt. More camps were constructed to absorb this additional number of refugees. Second, the Palestinian Liberation Organization (PLO) took advantage of the outcome of the war to assert an increasing political and military role. In September 1970, the Jordanian government launched an attack known as "Black September" against refugee camps in response to Palestinian military activities in Jordan. Previously, during the late 1960s, Jordan's King Hussein had experienced increasing Israeli reprisals for the raids carried out against Israel by the fedayeen, or Arab commandos. As a result, the Jordanian government was on the verge of collapse, impelling Hussein to confront the Palestinian resistance organizations and ultimately expel them from Jordan.

The Black September confrontation triggered widespread fighting between governmental forces and the Palestinian resistance organizations. In the subsequent months, the guerrillas were pushed entirely out of Jordan and found themselves with freedom of action only in Lebanon. The result was not only the relocation of the PLO power base to Lebanon, but also the consolidation of Palestinian presence there, which will be the focus of the next chapter.

Notes

1 The Palestinian narrative maintains that the Arab refugees were forcibly expelled by Jewish forces or left in a panic flight to escape massacre and that they were helped on their way by occasional massacres, committed by Jewish forces, to keep them running. Palestinians cite the UNRWA figure of 3,469,109 refugees (January 1998) as the minimum number, including 1,308,438 in the territories (548,874 in the West Bank and 759,564 in Gaza); some Palestinian sources argue that the total figure is as high as 4,900,000. See Joseph Alpher; Gabriel Ben-Dor; Ibrahim Dakkak; Yossil Katz; Herbert C. Kelman; Ghassan Khatib; Moshe Maoz; Nadim Rouhana; Yezid Sayyigh; Zeev Schiff; Shimon Shamir; Khalil Shikaki. Concept paper: "The Palestinian Refugee Problem and the Right of Return," *Middle East Policy* 6 (3) (1999), p. 167.
2 Robert I. Friedman, *Zealots for Zion* (New York: Random House, 1992), p. 197.
3 This position was sanctioned by UN Resolution 194 (III) of December 11,

1948, which states: "Refugees wishing to return to their homes and live at peace with their neighbors should be permitted to do so at the earliest practicable date and that for refugees choosing not to return, compensation should be paid by the governments or authorities responsible." See Nur Masallah, *The Palestinian Refugee Problem: Israeli plans to resettle the Palestinian refugees 1948–1972* (Ramallah: Palestinian Diaspora and Refugee Center, Shaml, 1996), p. 2.

4 Peter Sluglett and Marion Farouk Sluglett, *The Times Guide to the Middle East* (London: Times Books, 1991), p. 210.
5 Sybilla G. Thicknesse, *Arab Refugees: A Survey of Resettlement Possibilities* (London: Royal Institute for International Affairs, 1949).
6 Ibid., p. 45.
7 Ibid., p. 46.
8 Masallah, *The Palestinian Refugee Problem*, p. 2.
9 Jalal al-Husseini, "UNRWA and the Palestinian Nation-Building Process," *Journal of Palestine Studies* 29 (2) (2000), p. 51.
10 Martin Gilbert, *The Arab–Israeli Conflict* (London: Weidenfeld and Nicolson, 1992), p. 54.
11 Ibid., p. 54.
12 Ibid.
13 In Donald Neff, "US Policy and the Palestinian Refugees," *Journal of Palestine Studies* 18 (1) (Autumn 1988), p. 104.

3

The Palestinian Factor in the Lebanese Conflict

Lebanese officials showed lukewarm signs of support for the Arab cause, translating these into token military action in northern Palestine when the Arab–Israeli war formally broke out on May 15, 1948, after Zionist leaders proclaimed independence and set up the State of Israel. The pro-Western Lebanese government responded nonchalantly to the creation of a Jewish state, expressing worry about the influx of large numbers of Palestinian refugees, most of them Muslims, into a country already tormented by deep sectarian cleavages. Nonetheless, of all Arab nations, Lebanon was second only to Jordan in admitting Palestinians. However, after the war the Israeli authorities refused to allow them back, thus, transforming them into de facto permanent residents of Lebanon, where they took full part in the country's social and economic life.

From the beginning, given the precariousness of the Lebanese confessional political and social make-up, it was never going to be possible to address the problem of the political rights of the refugees in Lebanon. Jureidini and McLaurin note: "Even leaving aside the political repercussions of absorption, the potential total collapse of the confessional balance in Lebanon prevented any serious consideration of absorption of Palestinians by proffering nationality."[1]

However, despite reservations and concerns felt by Lebanese leaders, it was President Bishara El-Khuri who first welcomed the refugees mandating that they be given food, shelter and medical care. Even the Maronite Patriarch Antun Arida launched a call to all believers to assist their Palestinian brothers.[2] During this period, relations between the Lebanese and the Palestinians were characterized by a remarkable cooperation and harmony. By the mid-1950s, Lebanon was perceived as Israel's one harmless Arab neighbor, a state that, since 1949, had not taken part in the Arab–Israeli wars and would perhaps improve relations and even make peace if it were up to the country's Christians. But in Lebanon, the Maronite community's standing was being eroded and Israel, as a supporter of the status quo, could only offer discreet aid to its friends.[3] Still, despite the influx of Palestinian refugees and despite Lebanon's alignment internationally with the rest of the Arab world in dealing with the Arab–Israeli conflict, Lebanon did not threaten Israel's security or national interests.

Initially impoverished, fragmented, dispirited and without adequate leadership to address their concerns, the Palestinian refugee community was quiescent until the mid-1960s. While many Palestinians in Lebanon lived in refugee camps, others took an active role in the economic and intellectual life of the country.

In Lebanon, President Charles Helou's term (1964–70) coincided with the renewal of the Arab–Israeli conflict. The first Arab summit in Cairo endorsed the establishment of a Palestinian politico-military organization, which became known as the Palestine Liberation Organization (PLO), to organize the Palestinian people in their struggle against Israel.

During the 1960s, the Lebanese–Israeli border began to prove troublesome, thanks to the growing activities on its soil of Palestinian guerrilla groups. The Fatah, or victory movement, originally formed in 1959, became militarily active toward the end of 1964 in the shadow of the Arab cold war. Fatah constituted a major change in the policy adopted by Palestinian refugees, since it introduced an aggressive military dimension to the already progressing political movement. The considerable increase of anti-Israel Palestinian incursions, initiated from Jordan and Lebanon, prompted massive Israeli retaliation that destabilized the sovereign existence of the two countries and created an atmosphere of instability in Lebanon.

In the aftermath of the 1967 Six Day War, the Palestinians began to play a fundamental role in eroding the stability of Lebanon's regime. Until then, Lebanon had managed to remain relatively detached from the Arab–Israeli dispute, with the exception of its limited participation in the 1948 war and the stationing of the refugees on its soil. Domestically, the Palestinians did not threaten to destabilize the Lebanese system of "compromise politics," which rested on a stable equilibrium of interests."[4] However, the refusal of the Lebanese political leadership to commit its troops to the 1967 war enraged both Syria and many Lebanese Muslims. In addition, the Israeli Army's overwhelming victory and the unequivocal support provided to Israel by the United States following the outbreak of war mobilized the large Palestinian refugee camp population and its militias, igniting both Palestinian and Arab nationalist feeling. Given the crushing defeat of the Arab armies and the PLO's increasing awareness that the Arab regimes would subordinate the issue of a Palestinian homeland to each of their national interests, the PLO recognized that it needed to achieve independence from the Arab regimes in order to fulfill its nationalist goal.[5]

The Palestinian Factor in the Lebanese Conflict

With an increase in Lebanon's Palestinian population, from roughly 140,000 to over 240,000, Lebanon now had the second largest refugee population among the other Arab countries bordering Israel.[6] Fedayeen, Arab commandos, infiltrating from neighboring Syria, began launching raids across the Lebanon–Israel border with increased regularity, especially after the 1969 Cairo Agreement condoned such behavior.[7]

Lebanese Army attempts to regulate the Palestinian armed movement in the country were widely opposed by the Muslim and leftist leadership. In November 1969, following a series of clashes between Palestinians and the Lebanese Army, the Lebanese government was compelled under internal and external pressures to conclude the Cairo Agreement. The immediate effects of this accord were to allow the PLO to take military action without Lebanese regulation, and to acknowledge many important social rights for the Palestinians, such as the right to employment. The PLO assumed the responsibility of managing the affairs of the Palestinian community in the country.[8]

In September 1970, Jordan's King Hussein evicted the PLO from Jordan, whereupon its leadership and guerilla base relocated to Lebanon, where the Cairo Agreement endorsed their presence. This influx of several hundred thousand Palestinians upset Lebanon's delicate confessional balance and polarized the country over the Palestinian issue.[9]

Most important for Lebanon, however, was the ascendant activism that emerged among the Palestinians and which coincided with rising protests and discontent that manifested itself among the Muslim lower classes in Lebanon as well as in the middle strata, both of which had been virtually shut out of the political system. Hence, the movement for social change quickly became linked with the Palestine liberation movement. During that period, the PLO gained political and military power in Lebanon, and it increasingly touched off a resonance of sympathy from Sunni Muslims, who among all Lebanese confessions were the most enthusiastic about the existence of Palestinian resistance on Lebanese soil. Sunni Muslim support was a consequence of the inadequacy of their own recruitment into the Lebanese political system and because they had "their own homegrown grievances against the institutionalized domination of their state apparatus by the Maronites."[10]

Although the Lebanese state was not able to deter the armed Palestinians without upsetting the Muslims, right-wing Christians thought they could act to protect the Lebanese entity. They resented the Palestinians as a new community of Muslims and especially their "state within a state," which threatened to overthrow the Maronite-dominated political system. The Maronites reacted by establishing and training their own militias to counter the Palestinians.[11]

The sectarian structure of the Lebanese political system in which

Christian Maronites were previously dominant prevented the acceptance of Palestinians into Lebanese society. As detailed on pp.5–6, this society is shaped by the variety of its confessional groups. The Palestinians that resided in Lebanon prior to the civil war were composed of primarily Sunni Muslims (85%) and secondarily non-Maronite Christians (15%). In the case of the Palestinian Muslims, most were not legal citizens of the state.[12]

The presence of Palestinian refugees shifted the Muslim–Christian demographic balance in favor of the Muslims, which threatened the Maronite population; it also presented the host regime with additional social, political and economic challenges. According to the 1932 census (the last census taken in Lebanon), Christians slightly outnumbered Muslims, and the Maronites constituted the largest Christian sect.[13] By the mid-to late-1970s, however, it was estimated that the Muslims had surpassed the Christians in number due to higher Muslim birth rates.[14] This demographic change concerned the Maronites, who feared that Lebanon would be converted into a Muslim state if the Muslims increased their political representation. This fear reinforced the Maronites' insecurity, which stemmed from their minority status in the broader Arab world. In this regard, the Sheikh Farid Elias al-Khazen[15] contends that:

> To the extent that the PLO was perceived as a menace to communal interests and security, it provoked a populist reaction commensurate with that perception of threat. The most intense was expressed by the Kataeb (Phalange) Party. In a way, to be Kataeb was to oppose PLO aggression.

He adds that:

> Maronite reaction was a response to PLO insensitivity to Maronite communal sensitivities, which had been shaped by centuries of rebellion in Lebanon's mountains and valleys. To the extent that the Maronites viewed Lebanon as their last refuge after centuries of persecution and insecurity, they were not willing to share that refuge with a people also looking for refuge in the age of the nation-state.

The Palestinians' strong political and military presence in Lebanon during the 1970s, often referred to as a "state within a state," came at the expense of large segments of the Lebanese population. Of all communities, the overlap between the Maronite *raison de communaute* and *raison d'état* was comparatively the most spontaneous. Hence, their hostility toward the Palestinians, for their exploitation of the internal contradictions of the Lebanese society to their own ends: "We have no desire to throw these people into the sea, or to annihilate them. All we ask of them is to start looking for another land to settle on, outside the Lebanese territory."[16]

Lebanon's religiously and ideologically divided political system failed to

The Palestinian Factor in the Lebanese Conflict

cope with the consequences of armed Palestinian presence and overbearing Israeli punishment. Israel, by staging pre-emptive and punitive raids, reduced PLO pressure on its own border but played into the hands of those who sought to weaken the Lebanese state further and transform it into an entity far less acceptable to Israel.[17] In 1977 and 1978, Israel's preoccupation with the Palestinians in southern Lebanon overshadowed interest in the Lebanese crisis as a whole. Israel built an elaborate defense system along the Lebanese border, supported by three enclaves of Major Saad Haddad's South Lebanon Army – Israel's proxy militia in the southern part of the country – and struck Palestinian targets in Lebanon.

In March 1978, the heavy casualties and Israel's obvious vulnerability persuaded the Israeli government to launch the massive Litani operation. The operation had several important consequences: Haddad's territory became a continuous strip along the Israeli border; a large Shi'ite element was added to Haddad's militia and to the population they controlled; and the United Nations Interim Force in Lebanon – UNIFIL – was introduced to the region.

But neither the UN, nor Israeli strikes and commando raids, were able to stem the growth of cross-border PLO operations. Thus, on June 6, 1982, the Israeli Army moved into Lebanon to drive out the PLO in "Operation Peace for Galilee," a massive military invasion aimed at destroying the PLO's military and political power base in Lebanon. However, by the end of the second day of the invasion, the Israeli Army had already proceeded far beyond its self-proclaimed twenty-five mile limit and was on its way toward Beirut. By mid-June, Israeli troops had captured the capital and surrounded 6,000–9,000 Palestinian guerrilla fighters who had taken up positions amid the civilian population of West Beirut. Eventually the PLO bowed to American pressure and agreed to evacuate the city to a number of Middle East destinations – though even after this ejection and the collapse of most PLO institutions in the country, some Palestinian forces continued to be deployed in the north and the Bekaa Valley.

Moreover, when they left on August 21, 1982, the armed guerillas also left the Palestinian people behind trapped in the refugee camps and in an almost destitute status. The exodus left the Palestinian camps without armed protection, making them easy targets for right-wing Christian militiamen. Two days after the assassination of President-elect Bashir Gemayel, elements of the Lebanese Forces entered the Sabra and Shatila camps where, over a three-day period in September 1982, they slaughtered several thousand civilians.[18]

The following term, on May 9, 1983, a split occurred in Fatah, one that had a profound impact on the political and organizational situation in the camps of Lebanon. The Fatah rebellion faction, led by Abu Musa, gained the support of Syria and engaged in armed confrontation with loyalist

The Palestinian Factor in the Lebanese Conflict

forces in northern Lebanon and the Bekaa Valley. These confrontations ended with the defeat of the loyalists led by PLO Chairman Yasser Arafat, who had returned to Lebanon to direct the battles, and Palestinian evacuation from the camps near Tripoli. Meanwhile, the Fatah dissidents joined with the other opposition groups to form the Damascus-based National Salvation Front (NSF).[19] They were able – with Syrian support – to rebuild their bases in the camps of Beirut and some camps in southern Lebanon following the Israeli withdrawal from parts of the south.

By 1984, with Syrian assistance, the Shi'ite Amal militia controlled West Beirut, reigning over the many Sunnis there. But its paramountcy soon decayed. Moreover, the militia – the military wing of "Harakat al-Mahroumin," the political movement of the deprived founded by Imam Musa Sadr – held growing fears about pro-Arafat loyalist infiltration among the Palestinian population and armed elements resurfacing in the battered refugee camps of Sabra, Shatila and Bourj al-Barajneh. This resurgence rekindled bitter memories of pre-1982 PLO behavior, and for Amal and Syria alike, the PLO challenge became an obsession.

On May 20, 1985, after mounting friction, Amal and the Shi'ite Sixth Brigade of the Lebanese Army launched a war against the Palestinian camps in Beirut and southern Lebanon. This "War of the Camps," which was ostensibly designed to liquidate any and all remaining pro-Arafat Palestinian forces still in the country, rearranged alliances within the camps. The NSF and Amal, both Syrian allies, were on opposite sides, with the NSF undertaking the defense of the camps against Shi'ite Amal's indiscriminate attacks. Amal's unrelenting siege, during which hundreds of Palestinians died, continued for over two years, when it was finally lifted under Syrian pressure shortly after the beginning of the Palestinian uprising in the Occupied Territories.

The War of the Camps then gave way to a period of intra-Palestinian conflict. Now that Amal's siege was over, loyalist and opposition forces battled it out in the Shatila refugee camp in Beirut. The conflict ended with the removal of loyalist forces from Beirut and their redeployment in the camps of southern Lebanon. At the end of this period, the refugee camps of southern Lebanon (Rashidieh, al-Bass, Bourj al-Shamali, Ain al-Hilweh, and Mieh Mieh) were controlled by Fatah and loyalist contingents of the PLO. Meanwhile, the refugee camps in Beirut (Bourj al-Barajneh, Shatila, Mar Elias) and northern Lebanon (Baddawi and Nahr al-Barid) came under the control of the NSF – though both groups maintained a presence in all camps. Meanwhile, the War of the Camps also resulted in the withdrawal of the Popular Front for the Liberation of Palestine (PFLP) from the NSF and its alliance with the Democratic Front for the Liberation of Palestine (DFLP).

As a major military force, the PLO was essentially finished in Lebanon,

The Palestinian Factor in the Lebanese Conflict

but it had some influence on Lebanese developments as a result of the magnitude of the refugee problem that still constrained the government. Therefore, the official Lebanese-Palestinian dialogue formally resumed in the atmosphere of openness that followed the 1989 Ta'if Accord.

After years of lack of contact, the first official meeting took place at the Arab foreign ministers' meeting in Cairo in mid-May 1991 between Lebanese Foreign Minister Fares Boueiz and PLO Political Department head Farouk Qaddumi. The two men agreed to resume the dialogue in Lebanon, and a Lebanese ministerial committee headed by Defense Minister Muhsin Dallul, and including Brigadier General Nabih Farhat, was created to take charge of the dialogue. The Cairo meeting was followed by two sessions in Beirut: a political meeting between Boueiz and Qaddumi; and a procedural session between General Farhat and Salah Salah, an official of the Leadership of Palestinian National Action in Lebanon.

A three-point agenda was discussed at the Salah-Farhat meeting: (1) the Palestinian military presence in Lebanon; (2) the security situation in the camps; and (3) the social and civil rights of Palestinians in Lebanon. This was followed by meetings between Defense Minister Dallul and Salah. According to the Palestinian version of events, an agreement, never published, was reached whereby the Palestinians would hand over their heavy and medium weaponry and redeploy Palestinian military personnel inside the refugee camps, in exchange for the Lebanese government's agreement to give the Palestinians civil and social rights (short of citizenship and eligibility for government positions).[20] At all events, Palestinian weapons were handed over and military personnel withdrew into the camps, with limited skirmishes taking place east of Sidon.

On June 27, 1991, the Lebanese Army took up positions in Sidon and the rest of the south. Over 60 people were killed, 150 were wounded and 450 Palestinians were taken prisoner. Despite this heavy toll, most Palestinian fighters held their fire and withdrew to the nearby Ain al-Hilweh refugee camp. A few days later, and for the first time since the inception of Palestinian militancy in 1965, the PLO forces willingly surrendered their heavy and medium weapons to the Lebanese authorities.

In the wake of these developments, a new Lebanese ministerial committee, composed of Labor and Social Affairs Minister Abdullah Amin and Agriculture Minister Shawqi Fakhuri, was formed to conduct the dialogue. The Palestinians, meanwhile, responding to the ministerial committee's charge that there was no single Palestinian position, formed a new unified Palestinian committee including Salah (representing the Leadership of Palestinian National Action) and Fadl Shururu (representing the NSF). At the first meeting in September 1991, the Palestinian delegation submitted to the ministerial committee a memorandum entitled "The Civil and Social Rights of the Palestinian People," but the Lebanese committee requested more time to study the Palestinian demands, and the dialogue never resumed.[21]

It has been suggested that the indefinite suspension of the talks may be linked to the formation, not long after the September meeting, of the multilateral Refugee Working Group following the Madrid Peace Conference of October 1991.[22] The Lebanese government may have wanted to see how the talks developed and to avoid making what it considered unjustified concessions.[23]

In sum, these developments resulted in the deployment of the Lebanese Army in south Lebanon and the establishment of checkpoints at the entrances to the four refugee camps there, which became subject to close surveillance. Internally, the camps of the south remained under the control of the loyalists.

The breakout of the 1991 Gulf War increased pressure on the PLO, whose sweeping support for Iraq alienated Saudi Arabia and the other Gulf States, and resulted in increasing despair among Palestinians. Their support for Iraqi leader Saddam Hussein was seen to justify Kuwaiti reprisal against Palestinians, with the Palestinian community in Kuwait shrinking from 600,000 in 1990 to 250,000 in August 1991.[24]

The absence of support from the Arab Gulf states after the Gulf War and the absence of opportunities for work there increased pressure on the PLO. In fact, Kuwaiti authorities' reprisals against the Palestinian community in Kuwait resulted in the emigration of some 300,000 Palestinians.

The gradual evolution of Arab states' policies in favor of a contractual peace with Israel did not grow out of a feeling of national pride or collective cohesiveness. Rather, it took place in an atmosphere of overall weakness, fragmentation and inferiority *vis-à-vis* Israeli and American power, which seemed able to impose a political settlement based on what – for the Arab world – was an unfavorable balance of power.[25] The triumph of the West over the Soviet Union, the patron of radical Arab regimes and movements, decisively confirmed this picture. Arab feelings of weakness and inferiority also stemmed from the reality of inter-Arab fragmentation.[26]

The disappearance of the Eastern Bloc as a source of aid and support for the PLO also aggravated the situation. Thus, the Palestinians were forced to enter negotiations with Israel, culminating with the 1993 Oslo Accords. While Palestinians welcomed the attainment of self-rule and the prospect of a state contained therein, the refugees in Lebanon had little reason for rejoicing. In fact, the accords did not directly mention the 1948 refugees, who constituted the majority of Palestinians in Lebanon. However, the disarray in the Palestinian movement as a whole, precipitated by the Oslo Accords, did not produce any military fighting among the Palestinian groups in Lebanon, though the propaganda war intensified. The height-

The Palestinian Factor in the Lebanese Conflict

ened tensions between the loyalist PLO groups and the opposition made any kind of real cooperation within the camps impossible, exacerbating the competition for resources and the unnecessary duplication of services.

The peace discussions ushered in, among other things, a new era of serious debate about the destiny of Palestinian refugees still residing in the Arab world. This occurred because the present Arab political context differed sharply from that of the 1950s and early 1960s. The setbacks of the previous three decades appeared to have made the Arabs more accommodating in their dealings with Israel. This in turn revived the question of resettling Palestinian refugees, an issue of direct concern to three Arab countries: Syria, Jordan and Lebanon.

Politically, by excluding the refugees, the Oslo Accords revived the issue of resettlement and increased prospects that resettlement would be imposed by force. The accords, therefore, stirred fear and concern among Lebanese, because no final Israeli–Palestinian settlement could be possible without a solution to the problem of Palestinian refugees.[27] The future of the sizable Palestinian community that has resided in Lebanon since its displacement in 1948 is still one of the most disruptive and pervasive issues in Lebanon today.

Notes

1. Paul A. Jureidini and Ronald. D. Mclaurin, "Lebanon after the War of 1982," in Edward Azar (ed.), *The Emergence of a New Lebanon: Fantasy or reality?* (New York: Praeger Publishers, 1984), p. 5.
2. In Annie Laurent and Antoine Basbous, *Guerres Secretes au Liban*, (Paris: Gallimard, 1987), p. 19.
3. Itamar Rabinovich, *The War for Lebanon, 1970–1985* (Cornell University Press: Ithaca and London, 1989), p. 105.
4. Malcolm Kerr, "Political Decision-Making in a Confessional Democracy," in Leonard Binder (ed.), *Politics in Lebanon* (Toronto: John Wiley & Sons, 1966), p. 209.
5. At that point, the Palestinians became aware that empty Arab nationalist slogans, in the image of the following statement, could not ensure their return: "The day of the realization of the Arab hope for the return of the refugees to Palestine means the liquidation of Israel" (Abd Allah Al-Yafi, Lebanese prime minister, April 29, 1966) in Martin Gilbert, *The Arab–Israeli Conflict* (London: Weidenfeld and Nicholson, 1992), p. 54.
6. Kamal Salibi, *Crossroads to the Civil War: Lebanon 1958–1976* (Delmar: Caravan Books, 1976), p. 26.
7. Elisabeth Picard, *Lebanon: A shattered country* (New York: Holmes & Meier Publishers, 1996), pp. 79–81.
8. Although most Westerners associate the PLO with the centrist Fatah organization led by Yasser Arafat, other Palestinian groups, often referred to as the

Palestinian rejectionists, were far more extreme than Fatah in both their goals and methods. Whereas the Marxist groups sought to promote social revolution, Fatah's goal was more nationalist in character. Thus, the Marxist Popular Front for the Liberation of Palestine (PFLP), led by George Habash; the Marxist Democratic Front for the Liberation of Palestine (DFLP), led by Naif Hawatmeh; the PFLP-General Command led by Ahmed Jabril; Saiqa, sponsored by the Syrian Ba'ath Party; and the Arab Liberation Front, sponsored by the Iraqi Ba'ath Party, all coexisted with Fatah in Lebanon, though not very peacefully. The rejectionist groups frequently organized their own attacks on Israel, often without Arafat's blessing after he became chairman of the PLO in 1969. See Brenda Seaver, "The Regional Sources of Power Sharing Failure: The case of Lebanon," *Political Science Quarterly* 115, (2) (2001), pp. 247–73.

9 In 1968, three major Maronite Christian parties, The Kataeb (Phalange Party), The National Liberal Party (NLP) and The National Block entered a coalition called "The Triple Alliance," despite their differences, to confront Palestinian presence in Lebanon.

10 Helena Cobban, *The PLO: People, power and politics* (Cambridge: Cambridge University Press, 1984), p. 47.

11 Michael Hudson, *Arab Politics: The search for legitimacy* (USA: Yale University, 1977), pp. 306–7.

12 William Harris, *Faces of Lebanon: Sects, wars, and global extensions* (Princeton: Princeton University Press, 1997).

13 Arnon Soffer, "Lebanon – Where Demography Is the Core of Politics and Life," *Middle Eastern Studies* 22 (1986): 197–205.

14 Elie Salem, "Lebanon's Political Maze: The search for peace in a turbulent land," *Middle East Journal* 33 (1979), pp. 444–63.

15 Farid al-Khazen, *The Breakdown of The State in Lebanon, 1967–1976* (London: I. B. Tauris & Co. Ltd., 2000), p. 83.

16 In *Bashir Gemayel's Foreign Policy* (Publications of The Bashir Gemayel Foundation, 1999), p. 12.

17 Itamar Rabinovich, *The War for Lebanon, 1970–1985* (Cornell University Press: Ithaca and London, 1989), pp. 106–7.

18 See Charles Winslow, *Lebanon: War and politics in fragmented society* (London and New York: Routledge, 1996); Robert Fisk, *Pity the Nation: Lebanon at war* (London: André Deutsch, 1989) for the war period 1975–89.

19 The members of the NSF were: Fatah-Uprising, PFLP, PFLP-GC, Palestine Liberation Front, Palestinian Popular Struggle Front and Saiqa.

20 Se, Edgar O'Balance, *Civil War in Lebanon, 1975–1992* (London: Macmillan, 1998), p. 212.

21 The memorandum was published in *Nidaa al-Watan* on June 23, 1999, "Memorandum on Palestinian social and civil rights." The memorandum was signed by "The Unified Palestinian Delegation" and dated August 12, 1991. It addressed the following topics: residency, work, freedom of movement, education and professional training, institutions, trade unions, reconstruction of the camps, displaced persons and democratic freedoms.

22 The question of the refugees was addressed in two ways; the first through a

multilateral working group under Canadian supervision. The second approach to the issue was to include it as an item on the agenda of the "final status" negotiations.
23 See Jaber Suleiman "The Current Political Organizational, and Security Situation in the Palestinian Refugee Camps of Lebanon," *Journal of Palestine Studies* 29(1) (Autumn 1999): 66–75.
24 See for example, Emile Habiby "Don't Blame the Victim," *New Outlook* (September–November 1990), pp. 22–8; and Ann Lesch, "Contrasting Reactions to the Gulf Crisis: Egypt, Syria, Jordan and the Palestinians," *Middle East Journal* (Winter 1991), pp. 30–50.
25 Fouad Ajami, *The Dream Palace of the Arabs* (NewYork: Pantheon Books, 1998), pp. 253–312.
26 Bruce Maddy-Weitzman, "The Inter-Arab System and the Arab–Israeli Conflict: Ripening for resolution," *Journal of International Affairs* 5(1) (2000).
27 According to the *Mideast Mirror*, October 13, 1999, and to *An-Nahar* newspaper, November 9, 1999, American officials have raised a number of proposals involving the transfer of Palestinian refugees in Lebanon to other countries in the region (Iraq, Gulf states, Jordan). If none of these plans work out, American officials will seek reluctantly to arrange the naturalization of most refugees in Lebanon.

4

Obstacles to Integration and Resettlement

The social conditions of the Palestinians in various Arab host countries were acceptable in the immediate decades after 1948 and varied proportionally to rights and restrictions accorded to Palestinians. While Palestinians were not essentially and meaningfully integrated in Arab host countries because of special provisions and practices prohibiting naturalization on political grounds, Palestinians were accommodated in these host countries rather than integrated since – with exception of Jordan – very few Palestinians were able to obtain citizenship in Syria, Egypt and the Gulf States. In Jordan, Palestinians constitute approximately 60 percent of the total population and 95 percent of them hold citizenship. They are a powerful force in the nation's economy and can work in any occupation of their choice; indeed, they have served as generals in the army and as prime ministers. Palestinians in Syria are integrated into society at all levels and rarely suffer discrimination in employment, ownership, or political activity. Although they are not eligible for citizenship, they enjoy full legal equivalency with local nationals in almost all areas, including employment and governmental services. There are, however, some restrictions on Palestinian property ownership and mobility in Syria, as well as tight controls over political activities. Elsewhere (Iraq and Egypt particularly), Palestinians have been subjected to harsh treatment and restrictions, but their numbers in those countries are much smaller than in Lebanon.

Nonetheless, a distinct Palestinian identity was maintained: The sense or feeling of "displacement" and "otherness" or "peoplehood" remains there – i.e., Palestinians *vis-à-vis* Syrians, Palestinians *vis-à-vis* Jordanians.[1]

Palestinian Integration

For the first few years following their arrival in 1948, and until 1958, Palestinians refugees were welcomed by both the Lebanese government

Obstacles to Integration and Resettlement

and population and given material and moral support. But their treatment subsequently deteriorated under President Fouad Chehab. The regime initiated an aggressive policy toward Palestinians. The Lebanese state has kept pressure on them both within and out of the camps. The Lebanese government – out of conviction that granting Palestinians civil rights would be one step toward their permanent resettlement in the country – has initiated a series of restrictive policies and regulations aimed at encouraging as many Palestinians to leave the country as possible. Early governmental response was that the Palestinians should not be allowed to stay indefinitely in the country; Lebanese authorities refused to discuss any solution that would open the door for the Palestinians to become assimilated or naturalized. According to Lebanon's Prime Minister Rafik Hariri, "in the current peace process negotiations, to grant these civil and social rights, will be understood as settlement and Israel will benefit out of it."[2]

Consequently, not only are Palestinians denied basic refugee or immigrant rights,[3] but they have also been, in many cases, the victim of official discrimination, social derogation and exclusion.

First, there were the restrictions on political rights and naturalization. Palestinians have been excluded from public institutions of social life and from the legal rights and protections that the state affords its citizens. Officially, the Palestinian community does not call for Lebanese citizenship, although any of those who can acquire it do so. In the 1950s and 1960s, around 30,000 Palestinians were naturalized in Lebanon. After the civil war in 1994, citizenship was granted to another 27,000 who were mostly Shi'ite residents of southern border villages who had Palestinian refugee status.[4] Later, in 1995, a further 23,000 Sunni refugees were naturalized, though for reasons not made public – perhaps to balance out the Shi'ite numbers. Maronite protests ensured that the few remaining Palestinian Christians without Lebanese citizenship were then naturalized.[5]

Following this mass naturalization, both official and unofficial statements continued to proclaim that the Palestinian refugees constituted the greatest menace to national security. In this regard, the integration of Palestinian refugees has been seen as a major destabilizing force, one capable of upsetting the precarious sectarian balance of inter-group relations and possibly even bringing on a renewal of civil war.

Moreover, travel restrictions on Palestinians were always tight. Passports were rarely given, and the only documents issued by the government were temporary.[6] Palestinian residents in Lebanon have been placed under the jurisdiction of the General Bureau of Palestinian Affairs in the Ministry of Interior, which regulates their affairs relating to travel, personal status and movement from camp to camp. One of many accounts that demonstrate the difficult conditions of Palestinians states that:

> They live with the constant knowledge that they are not wanted where they are ... Palestinians from throughout Lebanon are moreover subject to the necessity of going through the Lebanese Surete Generale for identity papers and passports. Renewal of these documents has been the occasion for interrogations, imprisonment, the extortion of bribes and other forms of harassment ... [they are] the object of official oppression and discrimination.[7]

Then, on September 22, 1995, the Lebanese government made visas obligatory for those Palestinian refugees residing in Lebanon who also held Lebanese travel documents. This meant that Palestinians who left the country faced the possibility of being refused a re-entry visa to come back. However, that decision was annulled on January 12, 1999, when the government decided to treat Palestinian refugees who held Lebanese travel documents on the same basis as full Lebanese passport holders, facilitating their movement to and from foreign countries. However, the greatest majority remained stateless and are still treated as foreigners.

This leads to the second type of governmental restraints, which has to do with economic integration in the labor market – namely where Lebanese and Palestinians meet, interact and develop mutual interdependence. Palestinians are classified as "special case" category foreigners, along with Sri Lankans, Thais, Filipinos, Kurds and Syrians, who together constitute much of Lebanon's imported working class. Thus, Palestinian refugees, after 50 years of exile in Lebanon, have to compete in the job market with the above-mentioned categories of workers, like the Syrians, who do not need any prior authorization from the Ministry of Labor. Foreigners must obtain work permits and the law specifies more than 70 jobs to be carried out exclusively by Lebanese citizens. As a result, Palestinians are forced to work illegally and do unskilled jobs; mostly they work in small shops, usually within the camps, or do building or agricultural work (seasonal work).[8] These restrictions force them to work and to receive only a fraction of the salaries and the benefits that Lebanese receive for doing the same job.[9] Between 1982 and 1992, no work permits were issued to Palestinians.[10] Restrictions on Palestinian employment are no longer limited to the state; they are rapidly extending to the private sector. Rosemary Sayyigh points out that "even the main Sunni cultural institution (the Makassed), which readily offered employment and training to Palestinians in the early period, reversed this policy in the early 1970s."[11]

Second, and as a preventive measure to discourage them from remaining in the country, official policy has made it difficult for the younger generation of Palestinians to continue post-compulsory school studies, even if international assistance has helped to provide secondary school places for some. In the past, high levels of education enabled Palestinians to compete

Obstacles to Integration and Resettlement

for jobs even though they were disadvantaged as non-nationals. Educational achievement was also a source of collective pride and individual motivation – an interim substitute for a country and a passport. Palestinians in Lebanon are facing an educational crisis, however, after years of destruction and disruption. While the United Nations Relief and Works Agency (UNRWA) provides Palestinians in Lebanon with primary education, they find it extremely difficult to enter the government secondary schools, which is a prerequisite for access to the university, and Palestinians continue to be excluded from public institutions for higher education.[12] Normal public schools are closed to them, while private schools charge fees that are often beyond their means.[13] The resulting lack of education has jeopardized the economic independence and productivity of Palestinians.[14]

A third type of government restraint is legally enforced segregation in housing. Over half of the Palestinians in Lebanon live in twelve UNRWA registered refugee camps, geographically dispersed across the whole of Lebanon. Nonetheless, over 40,000 refugees live in camps not recognized by UNRWA, and an estimated 35,000 displaced in the Lebanese civil war are currently housed in temporary makeshift shelters.[15] Not only are Palestinians in Lebanon confined to well-defined, circumscribed and surveyed camps, but they are also prevented from carrying out even urgent reconstruction work in those camps, a situation which contributes to their insecurity. Restrictions on building and camp reconstruction have also resulted in severe overcrowding. Camp-dwellers are forbidden from building vertically and are severely restricted in the types of materials they can use to build their dwellings, to reflect the temporary nature of their homes.[16] Since 1992, refugees have been banned from bringing in any kind of building material into the camps – "not even stones to cover our graves," as one camp official put it.[17] Therefore, since the government has not shown the slightest interest in integrating the refugees, Lebanon remains the only host country where the quota of camp inhabitants is still higher than 50 percent.

Finally, and perhaps most important, Lebanese prejudices provide additional evidence, reinforcing Palestinians' perceptions of their situation in Lebanon. Almost by definition, Palestinians are held in low regard by Lebanese and are often subject of negative stereotypes, hatred and hostility. Palestinians also recognize the differences between Lebanese and Palestinians in social prestige and socio-economic conditions. According to Peteet, "there are several problems in distinguishing Palestinians from Lebanese and confining them to homogeneous enclaves."[18] However, until the late 1960s, the majority of Lebanese citizens did not manifest blatant prejudice or outright rejection of those Palestinian refugees who came to Lebanon in 1948, and who shared language and culture with their Lebanese hosts. In fact, many Palestinians have formed strong social and economic ties, through a long history of intermarriage and trade, to their host country. According to one Lebanese official, for example, fully one-quarter of third-generation Palestinians in Lebanon have one Lebanese parent.[19]

Although urban Palestinian camps, which were scattered all over Lebanese territory, had merged with surrounding Lebanese areas by the mid-1970s, Lebanon's official policy still contributed, through deliberate spatial containment, to creating and sharpening communal distinctions. During the 1950s, tight vigil by the army curtailed movement for Palestinians. Later, with the dissolution of state authority in the 1970s and 1980s, local Lebanese militias crafted and imposed boundaries where a fluidity of space and social relations once prevailed between Lebanese and Palestinians.[20] In post-war Lebanon, Palestinian refugees describe their lives in terms of abnormality. Aside from shortages of shelter, food, safety and access to medical care and education, they have constant doubts about the security of residence. Not only were Palestinians landscaped out of Palestine, but this erasure continues in exile. A Palestinian lawyer, echoing popular sentiment, has written that "there are those who believe that the group known as Palestinian refugees in Lebanon will stop existing within a few years."[21]

The refugee experience did not include the usual minority attributes of difference in language, religion and culture. The Palestinians learned early in their exile that refugee life entailed degradation and the humiliation of being exposed to the mockery of local inhabitants. By definition, Palestinians are held in low regard by Lebanese and are often subject of negative stereotypes, hatred and hostility.

Palestinian marginality is contingent, to some extent, on the concept of a Lebanese nation and society – however problematic that concept is – which excludes them. This negative identity held by their hosts has prompted some observers to characterize Lebanese society as "minestrone" rather than a "melting pot," and has encouraged the Palestinians to stress their culture, tradition and own identity.[22] According to Sayyigh, "Palestinians play little part in this new Lebanon. Marginalized politically, economically and socially, they constitute a sect without a recognized place in a sectarian society."[23]

Palestinian Resettlement

In spite of growing opposition and Beirut's declared position rejecting any permanent settlement of the estimated 400,000 Palestinian refugees in Lebanon, several politicians maintain that Lebanon will have to keep an indefinite number of refugees as part of a comprehensive solution to resettle the vast majority in other Arab countries, Israel and Western countries.[24] Under the "best" circumstances, it might be possible to ensure that 250,000 to 300,000 of them leave, but Lebanon will find itself compelled to absorb at least 100,000.[25] This prospect finds support among refugees themselves who stipulated in an opinion poll[26] that they are willing to accept settlement in Lebanon if it serves as a start to solving their problems (49%). And while 67 percent of those polled said they prefer to hold both Lebanese and Palestinian nationalities, 96 percent said they would refuse to leave Lebanon for any country other than Palestine. There is not much sympathy in Lebanon, at either the official or the street level, for the permanent settlement of a considerable number of Palestinians. In general, Lebanese authorities avoid raising this issue because it causes internal divisions – not about the principle of rejecting the settlement of Palestinians, but about the way in which this policy should be implemented. Some in Lebanon believe that the presence of the Palestinians here will create demographic, economic, social and sectarian disorder. More specifically, Lebanon's opposition to resettlement rests on several major alleged contentions:

Negation of the right of return

Opposition has come from all spectrums of society. Even the Lebanese Sunnis, who theoretically have most to gain by the assimilation of the mostly-Sunni Palestinians, oppose a permanent settlement. Former Lebanese Prime Minister Salim Hoss, himself a Sunni, justified this position on the grounds that it contradicted the Palestinian right to return home. By the same token, Lebanese President Emile Lahoud, a Maronite, emphasized this point in a 1999 address to Beirut community leaders: "We cannot accept a settlement without . . . the sacred right of return of Palestinian refugees to their land."[27] Other examples of this common political position include a statement by Hizbullah secretary-general Hassan Nasrallah, a Shi'ite:[28] "First, regarding resettlement plans, we are with the rest of the Lebanese and with the rest of the Palestinians in rejecting the resettlement plans, although the Palestinians are our dear brothers. The natural thing is for the Palestinians to return to their land in Palestine."

Economic Issues

Lebanon is the Arab country with the second highest population density in the Middle East, yet it has some of the fewest resources and wealth. It is historically a country of emigration, not a country of immigration and settlement – it has lost people as a result of war and the chronic poor economy. Lebanon also has its own displaced populations, which have yet to be allowed to return to their villages and towns. The settling of

Palestinian refugees would increase Lebanon's population by approximately 10 percent, representing a demographic change that simply could not be absorbed.[29] This contention is supported by statistical evidence from a UNDP poll showing that Lebanon already suffers a high rate of unemployment (25%) and that 60 percent of youths aged 22–29 have considered emigrating.[30]

Moreover, Lebanon's geographical area is very small in relation to its population. The area that can be settled and exploited, after eliminating the mountains and deep valleys, is very small. This makes it impossible to assimilate the Palestinian refugees, especially following the devastation inflicted by the civil war. In 2000, former minister Michel Edde[31] called it "impossible" for Palestinian refugees to settle in Lebanon due to the "very difficult" economic situation and "people emigrating due to the high rate of unemployment."

Political and historical issues

Granting the refugees sanctuary was originally undertaken as a humane, emergency measure following their exodus from Palestine in 1948; it was never intended to be permanent. The situation of the Palestinian refugees in the existing camps in Lebanon is basically different from their situation in some Arab countries where they live, work and enjoy medical and educational security.[32] After more than 50 years, Lebanese see themselves as having paid a much higher price for the Palestinian cause than any other country. There are harsh memories of the civil wars of the 1970s and 1980s in which the Palestinians are blamed for dragging the country into bloodshed. Lebanese feel they cannot be asked to pay more in the form of the consequences incumbent on settling the Palestinians in Lebanon. In this regard, former Foreign Affairs Minister Fares Boueiz points out: "Lebanon was never before, nor is now capable of dealing with this large number of Palestinians – it is not right to resolve the Palestinian problem by creating a Lebanese one."[33] Boueiz stressed that "Lebanon cannot under any circumstances give citizenship to the Palestinians."

The Maronite patriarch, Cardinal Nasrallah Sfeir, concurs with Boueiz, by expressing his uncompromising rejection of *"tawtin,"* or implantation: "I fear that Lebanon will have to pay a dire price for peace in the region . . . no one can impose implantation on the Lebanese people."[34] This point was also stressed by Information Minister Ghazi Aridi,[35] who declared: "We refuse any implantation . . . This is a basic Lebanese national issue on which we cannot make any compromise."[36]

Obstacles to Integration and Resettlement

Demographic issues

Lebanon is a multi-confessional country with nineteen officially recognized sects, though the majority of Lebanese belong to three main sects: Muslim, Christian and Druze. As noted earlier, the Lebanese sectarian structure is very delicate. Palestinians citizenship would further skew the already shaky balance between Christians and Muslims, and between Sunni and Shi'ite Muslims.[37] Any imbalance would have a major political, social, economic and security impact.

Granting Lebanese nationality to the Palestinians – the majority of whom are Sunni Muslims – would upset the delicate social balance. The Christians anticipated that the largely Muslim refugees might threaten their economic and political dominance and assume demographic majority. The Christians feared, and still fear, that a large Palestinian presence could upset the sectarian balance and political status quo by serving as a focal point for the growing discontent of Lebanon's Muslims and their eventual political mobilization for a greater share of power and national resources. Lebanon's Shi'ites concur, out of fear that Palestinians will tilt the Muslim Lebanese balance in the wrong direction.[38] The present government proclaims that the Palestinian refugees constitute the greatest menace to national security. The large number of mostly Muslim refugees is seen as threatening to destroy the entire political system of their host country.

As mentioned earlier, there is a paucity of large-scale research on the relations between religious affiliation, demographic characteristics and social attitudes on the one hand, and attitudes toward the permanent settlement of Palestinians in Lebanon (an exception being the evidence provided from a cross-sectional survey of Lebanese groups) on the other.[39] These connections have become very relevant over the past few years because both government and society have placed an increasing emphasis on the issue of refugee resettlement in Lebanon. The intensity of anti-Palestinian feelings, judged by the intensity and salience of hostile attitudes publicly expressed, prompted one journalist to characterize Lebanese attitudes toward Palestinians as ranging between two poles: indifference at one level and negativeness at the other, with negativism varying between active hostility and passive dislike.[40]

Having examined basic dimensions that characterize Lebanese–Palestinian social, economic and political relations, we may now focus on placing them in an appropriate theoretical context for empirical treatment.

Notes

1   Nasir Aruri, and Samih Farsoun,"Palestinian Communities and Arab Host Countries," in Khalil Nakhle, and Elia Zureik (ed.), *The Sociology of*

Obstacles to Integration and Resettlement

Palestinians (London: Croom Helm, 1980), pp. 112–146; Marie Arneberg, *Living Conditions Among Palestinian Refugees Displaced in Jordan* (Oslo: Fafo draft report, 237, 1997); Laurie Brand, "Palestinians in Syria: The politics of integration," *The Middle East Journal*, 42(4) (Autumn 1988), pp. 621–38; Rex Brynen, "Imagining a Solution: Final status arrangements and Palestinian refugees in Lebanon," *Journal of Palestine Studies* 26(2) (Winter 1997); Uri Davis, "Citizenship Legislation in the Syrian Arab Republic," *Arab Studies Quarterly* 18(1) (Winter 1996), pp. 29–48.

2. Cited in Hussein Chaaban, "Palestinian Refugees in Lebanon and the Host State Regulations," www.prc.org.uk/english/refugees-lebanon.
3. Charles Westin, "The Effectiveness of Settlement and Integration Policies Toward Immigrants and Their Descendants in Sweden," Geneva: Migration Branch, International Labor Office, *International Migration Papers* 34 (2001).
4. Newsletter, Palestinian Diaspora and Refugee Center, Shaml, February 6, 1997.
5. Julie Peteet, "Identity Crisis: Palestinians in Post-War Lebanon," Worldwide Refugee Information, Washington, D.C.: US Committee for Refugees, www.refugees.org (1999), p. 24.
6. Decree 319, issued on August 2, 1962 in order to regulate Palestinian presence, equates Palestinians with foreigners and gives Lebanese residence permits and temporary travel documents to those Palestinians who fled their homes in 1948 and who are registered by UNRWA.
7. Rashid Khalidi, "The Palestinians in Lebanon: Social repercussions of Israel's invasion", *Middle East Journal* (Spring, 1984), pp. 259–60.
8. Mohamemed Tahri and Maria Donato, "Refugees also have rights: Palestinian refugees in Lebanon and Jordan", EMHRN Mission Report, published by the Euro-Mediterranean Human Rights Network, (17–18 September 2000), p.22.
9. Steven Edminster, *Trapped on All Sides: The marginalization of Palestinian refugees in Lebanon* (Washington, D.C.: US Committee for Refugees, 1999), p. 14.
10. Rosemary Sayyigh, *Too Many Enemies: The palestinian experience in Lebanon* (London: Zed Books Ltd, 1994).
11. Rosemary Sayyigh, "Palestinians in Lebanon: Status Ambiguity, Insecurity and Flux," *Race and Class* (Winter 1988), p. 23.
12. Sayyigh, *Too Many Enemies*, 1994, pp. 104–5.
13. T. Hammarberg, "The Palestinian Refugees: After Five Decades of Betrayal – Time at Last?" Swedish Ministry of Foreign Affairs, Stockholm, 2000.
14. The Norwegian report estimated that 20 percent of the refugees' adult population is illiterate, and 40 percent of students quit school before the age of 11 either due to lack of motivation or poverty. See Zayan, op. cit, 2000.
15. Mahmood Abbas, "The Socio-Economic Conditions of The Palestinians in Lebanon: The housing situation of the Palestinians in Lebanon," *Journal of Refugee Studies* 10(3) (1997), pp. 380–1
16. Wadie Said, "The Palestinians in Lebanon: The rights of the victims of the Palestinian–Israeli peace process," *Columbia Human Rights Law Review* 30(2) (Spring 1999), p. 34

Obstacles to Integration and Resettlement

17. "In the camps, sheer frustration: Palestinian refugees," *The Economist*, September 8, 2001.
18. Julie Peteet, "From Refugees to Minority: Palestinians in post-war Lebanon," *Middle East Report* (July–September 1996), p. 28.
19. Rex Brynen, "Imagining a Solution."
20. Pauline Cutting, *Children of the Siege* (London, Pan Books, 1988).
21. Suheil al-Natour, "The Legal Status of Palestinian Refugees in Lebanon," in Refugees in the Middle East, Nordic NGO Seminar (Oslo: Norwegian Refugee Council, March 26–27, 1993).
22. Ulrich Koltermann, "Who Really Wants Them? Palestinians in Lebanon fed up with being a bargaining chip," *The Jerusalem Times*, June 27, 1997.
23. Rosemary Sayyigh, "Palestinians in Lebanon: Harsh present, uncertain Future," *Journal of Palestine Studies* 25(1) (Autumn 1995), p. 40.
24. Khalil Fleihan, "Taalik ala ziyarat amin ashuun alkharijiah fi alitihad al urubi" (Comments on the Secretary for Foreign Relations in the European Union's Trip to the Middle East), *An-Nahar*, Beirut, March 28, 2000.
25. Nada Abd-al-Samad, "Palestinian Settlement In Lebanon," *Al-Majallah* London, 9–15 April 1995; Emile Khoury, "Tawtin al Filastiniin fi lubnan" (Settling Palestinians in Lebanon), *An-Nahar*, Beirut, February 1, 2000.
26. *Al-Quds*, "Poll shows half of Palestinian refugees prepared to settle there," October 24, 1999.
27. *An-Nahar*, Beirut, July 29, 1999.
28. Nasri Hajjaj, "Interview with Hizbullah secretary–general Hassan Nasrallah," *Al-Ayam*, Ramallah, (January 1, 2000), p. 15.
29. This could mean that 40–45 percent of total Lebanese territory cannot be exploited and may result in increasing the population density, possibly reaching as high as 632/km². This is a huge figure, especially compared to countries like Iraq (47/km²) and Australia (2/km²).
30. Gabi Habib, "The Naturalization Decree Strips Lebanese Identity," *An-Nahar*, December 7, 1999, p. 24.
31. *The Daily Star*, December 30, 2000.
32. An interview with Lebanon's Foreign Minister Fares Boueiz, *Journal of Palestine Studies* 24(1) (1994), pp. 130–2.
33. M. Chahine, "Those Left Behind," *The Middle East*, 252 (January, 1996), pp. 17–19
34. *An-Nahar*, "*Al-Tawtin Yastather Bi Ihtimam Al-diman*," (Palestinian implantation worries Dimaan) Beirut, July 29, 1999.
35. *Time International*, 157(12) (March 2001), pp. 27–6.
36. In addition to increased attention to the Palestinian refugee question in Lebanon, a conference on Palestinian resettlement was held in 1999, "Lebanese Identity: Between Naturalization and Implantation," at the University of Saint Esprit, Kaslik, on November 11. An academic workshop titled "Opposing Resettlement" was also held at Saint Joseph University, organized by the Research Center for Arab Law, Beirut on 26 November. It grouped prominent Lebanese figures and even the prime minister. This trend received additional support with the announcement that Lebanese clerics of all sects intended to hold conference to take a harsh stance on the matter on July 29.

37 Though Lebanon's constitution allocates public offices on the basis of a 50:50 ratio of Christians vs. Muslims, it is commonly accepted that the Muslims now constitute a majority in the country.
38 *The Economist*, 323 (7758) (May 9, 1992).
39 See Khashan, "Palestinian Resettlement in Lebanon," 1994.
40 Jihad Zeine, *As-Safir*, author interview, Beirut, December 12, 1994.

Adverse living conditions of Palestinian refugees in Lebanon, as well as official discrimination by Lebanese authorities and neglect by the international community, do not hamper Palestinian refugees from voicing support for the Intifada.

While Hizbullah still mulls over its options in the wake of Israel's withdrawal from Lebanon, the 350,000 Palestinian refugees represent a potential source of renewed tension of political activism.

Palestinian refugee children carrying arms to demonstrate their high degree of mobilization and support for the *Intifada* in the Palestinian territories.

Mounir Madqah, Yasser Arafat's militia commander in the Ain al-Hilweh camp. In his statements to the press, Maqdah dwells on the Palestinian right of return and expresses his opposition to peace with the Jewish state.

Palestinian refugee children who have no playgrounds can only play in the narrow alleys and streets inside the camps.

Western media reporters visiting the Shatila refugee camp whose residents are slated for transfer elsewhere. Lebanese government postwar reconstruction maps show the current camp areas as blank and as unnamed areas.

Hundreds of Palestinian refugees at the Ain al-Hilweh camp near the port city of Sidon in south Lebanon demonstrating and waving portraits in support of embattled Palestinian leader Yasser Arafat, whose ouster has been called for by Washington in the summer of 2002.

Palestinian refugee children sitting in front of a memorial to the victims of the 1982 massacre at the Sabra and Shatila refugee camps in Lebanon. Hundreds of civilians were slaughtered at Shatila and the neighboring Sabra camp on September 16–18, 1982. Ariel Sharon, who was Israel's Defense Minister at the time, is widely held to be responsible for allowing the massacre to take place.

Many Palestinian refugee youth prefer to emigrate from Lebanon, because they believe that the establishment of a Palestinian state is not a viable option. Feelings of despair and resentment are passed from generation to generation. There is much misery and a feeling of desperation among the youth.

Much of the destruction in the Shatila camp is still visible after 20 years. There is no potable water, and residents suffer from disease. Many children suffer psychological problems, and outbursts of aggression are common.

Lebanese high-ranking officials taking part in a demonstration in support of the Intifada and the Palestinians' right of return – an allusion to their undesirability on Lebanese soil.

Pro-Palestinian Lebanese politicians at the Mieh Mieh Palestinian refugee camp protesting against America's pro-Israel bias. The 400-strong demonstration was held at the camp during the summer of 2002, to express rejection of recent American calls for the expulsion of Palestinian President Yasser Arafat. Leaders from the PLO headed the crowd; they toured the camp carrying pictures of Arafat, shouting slogans supporting the Palestinian president and calling for the right of return for Palestinian refugees.

At the entrance of the Ain al-Hilweh camp, youths torch Israeli and US flags and burn effigies of Israeli Prime Minister Ehud Barak and right-wing opposition leader Ariel Sharon, to protest against Israel. Young Palestinian Mohamed al-Durra was killed, and his father gravely wounded, when they came under "Israeli" fire, September 30, 2000.

Palestinian gunmen involved in the brief clash between Fatah militia and Islamist factions inside the Ain al-Hilweh camp, August 2002.

A Palestinian guerrilla defending Fatah's headquarters at the main entrance of the Ain al-Hilweh camp on the outskirts of the Lebanese port city of Sidon after Islamists staged a surprise attack.

Palestinians displaying support for Hamas leader Sheikh Ahmad Yassin.

Thousands of Palestinians demonstrate in support of former Iraqi president Saddam Hussein.

Part II

Methodological Criteria: Studying Immigration, Discrimination and Integration

5
Measuring Attitudes toward Immigration and Immigrants

Part II lays out the procedural aspects of the fieldwork. The theoretical framework is elaborated and the concepts used to guide the investigation are operationalized in order to develop testable hypotheses.

Relevant Theoretical Considerations

The act of leaving one's native country and settling in another land has immediate and long-term consequences for both immigrants and members of immigrant-receiving nations. Immigration presents a range of challenges, and the challenge of managing immigration successfully – in ways that facilitate the achievement and well-being of immigrants, that benefit the country collectively and that produce the cooperation and support of members of the receiving society – is critical for nations and individuals.[1] These issues have been framed, academically, largely in terms of economics, politics and resource management. As a consequence, economists, sociologists, political scientists, demographers, historians and geographers have studied them extensively.[2]

While an estimated 80 million migrants – almost 2 percent of the world's population – live permanently or for long periods of time outside their countries of origin,[3] in most cases, and even in Europe, nations have seen harsh, often violent, reactions to these new minorities.[4] As Solomos and Wrench[5] indicate, "In many societies in contemporary Europe, questions about migration and the position of minorities are among the most hotly contested areas of social and political debate. Developments in Britain, France and Germany over the past decade have highlighted the volatility of the phenomenon and the ease with which it can lead to violent conflict." Even immigration that clearly and objectively benefits a nation as a whole does not necessarily have the same consequences for all segments of the population.[6]

Immigration may thus be perceived as threatening and undesirable by subsets of a population.[7] Opposition to immigration may vary systematically as a function of perceived competition across time and for different segments of the receiving society.[8] Many of the indigenous population continue to view the new minorities as not belonging – and this applies even to the growing numbers of the second- and third-generation immigrants who have lived only in the host nation. They view the new minorities as "a people apart" who violate traditional values and for whom they feel little sympathy or admiration. The result is that there is a tendency to discriminate against them.[9]

Discrimination comes about only when individuals or groups are denied equal treatment.[10] Both direct and indirect discrimination is involved.[11] Direct discrimination, where blatantly prejudiced people may oppose immigration categorically, is straightforward and sets up spatial boundaries of some sort to accentuate the disadvantage of immigrants. It occurs at points where inequality is generated, often intentionally; for example, when steps to exclude members of a certain group from a neighborhood, school, occupation or country are taken. A classical example is provided by surveys of black/white interracial contact in the United States. Scholars assert that whites accept blacks across a range of formal and informal settings. Preferred social distance or pro-integration sentiments among whites measured their acceptance concerning, for example, bringing a black person home for dinner, allowing blacks into the neighborhood and permitting interracial marriage.[12]

Indirect discrimination involves people with more subtle biases who may oppose the immigration of certain groups of people (i.e., stigmatized racial or ethnic groups) but justify their exclusion on the basis of reasons other than prejudice, such as economic reasons.[13] It operates when, for example, the inability to obtain citizenship restricts the opportunities of non-EU minorities in most institutions. It restricts their ability to get suitable housing, employment and schooling for children, or when a visa is required for travel to other EU countries. In short, the lives of non-citizens are severely circumscribed.[14] Castles contends that the newcomers are established as a problematic and stigmatized group, suitable for low-status jobs but not for citizenship.[15]

Wilpert goes further. She asserts that Germany's institutions, for example, are based on "a dominant ideology, which distributes rights according to ethnic origins."[16] The revealing comparison is between the almost two million *Aussiedler*,[17] or foreigners, and the *Gastarbeiter*, or guest workers/foreign workers. Officials often regard the former as kin on the thinnest of evidence, though since 1996 a language test must also be taken. *Aussiedler* readily become citizens and receive favorable government treatment. Long recognized as the largest single group of so-called non-

Germans dwelling in Germany, Turks have the most pressing practical claims to German citizenship, yet by law, it is denied to most of them.[18]

In the meantime, the second and even third generations of immigrants have become established in Germany, and the greater size and presence of the immigrant population has impacted upon public awareness of the situation. Children of foreign-born parents were educated and socialized entirely in Germany, without returning to their so-called homeland – a situation exemplifying the question of identity in and with the German society.[19] As Leslie Adelson notes, this situation is especially relevant to Turkish residents of Germany. Yet even third-generation Turks, who are at least as culturally "German" as the *Aussiedler*, are largely denied citizenship and given unfavorable treatment.

Over the course of time, both the position of the German government as well as the attitudes of the general population have served to create and define an identity for immigrant populations in Germany, based primarily on popular perception. "Instead of viewing the foreigners only in terms of their problems and their economic value, the German population should recognize the various foreign cultures which the migrant workers brought with them as an enrichment of German culture . . . Reiterating the position that the Federal Republic of Germany is not an immigration country has contributed to the general perception of foreigners as illegitimate intruders and a threat to German culture."[20]

The ethno-cultural understanding of citizenship in Germany – which grounds membership in the polity in cultural terms; that is, in terms of ancestry, custom and language – links the issue of immigrant incorporation to the question of acquisition of cultural and social competencies, solidarities and loyalties.[21] The central question thus becomes how to culturally incorporate immigrants into the German polity without endangering the national and social cohesion of German society. Within this context, the moral aspect of immigration – that is, the question of who is eligible for inclusion in the polity – immediately turns into a question of newcomers' loyalty and solidarity.[22]

The crucial point, then, is the intertwined relationship between solidarity (loyalty) and cultural difference. As a result of this interrelationship, the question of dual-citizenship in Germany has been treated as a question of dual (and conflicting) loyalties.[23] Once the maintenance of cultural difference is interpreted as a sign of non-solidarity and non-loyalty, the project of integration takes the form of a taming of cultural difference.

The task of integration in Germany's regulated economy and society is seen as the systematic coordination, regulation and modification of cultural diversity in the public domain so as not to endanger civil society.[24] Within this framework, Turkish immigrants' persistent ties with the homeland have come to be conceptualized as a major obstacle to their integration in German society. As a consequence, the notion of the "ghetto" is the dominant topic in the discourse on *Auslander* (foreigner) integration in Germany. The so-called cultural enclaves are considered to be the ultimate expression of this refusal and/or the German state's failure to manage cultural diversity so that it would not pose a threat to the solidarity of the imagined community. The spatial inscription of immigrants' presence in urban space by means of a ghetto image, and the fear of ghettos, are based on this metaphysics of sedentarism, which is responsible for the conceptualization of immigrant and diaspora populations "as a spatial and temporal extension of a prior, natural identity rooted in locality and community."[25]

Citizenship acquisition is a direct force, which affects immigrants' potential political influence and their mobility in the host country.[26] Citizenship acquisition signifies the shift of immigrants' allegiance and commitment to the receiving country, and therefore it also measures the extent to which immigrants are willing to become an integral part of the host society.

A study of immigration in the United States demonstrated that issues related to costs, benefits and meaning of naturalization are the most immediate considerations in immigrants' decisions to naturalize:[27]

First, citizenship grants immigrants certain political, civic and social rights and privileges to which permanent residents are not entitled. One of the most important privileges of citizens, which inspires immigrants to seek citizenship, is political rights; namely, the right to vote and run for public office, and therefore to influence political decisions and outcomes at the national, state and local levels which may have bearings on their lives.

Second, it is a widely held belief that many immigrants primarily pursue naturalization not for political rights, but for immigration benefits accompanying citizenship – easier and faster immigration of their relatives to the host country.

A third significant advantage of acquiring citizenship is the qualification for a passport; access to broader life opportunities is a fourth naturalization benefit. However, the researcher notes that while the value of citizenship in political rights, immigration benefits and international travel has remained stable over the past three decades, the specific marginal value of citizenship in the sphere of civic and social rights has diminished over time as additional privileges attached to permanent residence have increased.

Conversely, citizenship also entails costs. These comprise at least four types:

First are increased citizen obligations in the host country, which, in addition to universal obligations of all residents such as paying taxes and obeying laws, include the responsibilities to participate in the political process, to uphold the constitution, to serve in the military if necessary and to remain loyal to their adopted country during wartime.

Second, lost or reduced political, civic and social rights previously enjoyed as nationals in the country of origin. Third is a voluntary renunciation of their former nationality and of allegiance to their native land through oath, which, in some sense, can be considered as a psychological cost.

Finally, citizenship indicates the change of one's national identity, a change from a "foreigner" to, for example, an "American." The feeling about this identity change varies considerably from person to person. Some immigrants find it honorable to be an American, while others feel ambivalent or indifferent or even find it dishonorable, depending upon their sense of belonging and commitment to their native country.

Attitudes toward Immigration: Ethnocentrism and Multiculturalism

The relationship between the presence of an ethnic or racial group and the attitude held toward that group has been studied from different theoretical and methodological perspectives. One approach has been based on a model that regards inter-group competition for scarce resources, which may be economic or power related, to result in negative inter-group attitudes.[28]

In his survey of Canadian attitudes toward immigration, Tienhara found that opposition to immigration was greater during recession and attributed most to unemployment concerns.[29] A series of studies by Stephan[30] and his colleagues found that realistic threat, including perceived job loss, was a strong predictor of unfavorable attitudes toward immigrants. Using data obtained from the euro barometer, Quillian[31] indicated that perceived economic competition and threat were considered to be a joint function of the current economic situation in a country and the relative size of the immigrant group. In multicultural Canada, economic concerns and worries have been assigned a more important role than intolerance in determining the attitude toward immigration. This point receives support from a recent investigation that brought similar results using survey data in many studies on immigration and attitudes toward immigrants.[32]

A second approach to the study of the relationship between ethnic presence and ethnic attitudes can be found in investigations stemming from the contact hypothesis.[33] The contact hypothesis states that under certain conditions (participants of equal status, cooperative relations with acquaintance potential), contact with members of a group leads to positive attitudes. The contact hypothesis is consistent with the "mere exposure" hypothesis,[34] which postulates that repeated exposure to a given object results in familiarity with the object, which consequently leads to more positive attitudes toward it. According to both the contact and mere exposure hypotheses, ethnic presence leads to positive attitudes toward the group because of the potential for acquaintance with members of the group.

A number of studies from the US, Canada and Europe have shown that ethnic and racial tolerance is generally higher where contact with minority groups is relatively more likely. Williams, Hamilton and Ford[35] have reported lower levels of prejudice in US cities that are relatively more "integrated." Several studies in Canadian schools have related ethnic attitudes to ethnic composition. Reich and Purbhoo[36] found children in schools with a high – as compared with a low – percentage of "new Canadians" to be better in cross-cultural role-taking (but no different on a general measure of tolerance). Ziegler[37] found a positive relationship between "ethnic density" and preference for social diversity. George and Hoppe[38] discovered that white children in mixed (white and Native Indian) schools, as compared with children in all-white schools, were more likely to select non-whites as potential friends.

Kalin and Berry[39] analyzed the results of a Canadian national survey on ethnic attitudes conducted in 1974 with reference to objective information on the ethnic composition of respondents' neighborhoods, as revealed through data from the 1971 census of Canada. The survey had assessed familiarity with, and attitudes toward, seven ethnic groups (English, French, Native Indians, Germans, Ukrainians, Italians, Jews). The percentage presence of these groups in small geographic units (census tracts or area aggregates) of respondents' domicile was related to familiarity with, and attitudes toward, the seven groups. For familiarity, direct linear relationships were found with ethnic presence. With regards to attitudes, direct linear relationships (although somewhat weaker than for familiarity) were also found for six of the seven groups. A weak negative relationship was found for Native Indians. Kalin and Berry maintained that the most plausible explanation for these results were the contact and mere exposure hypotheses.

In a more recent study of multiculturalism in Canada, the authors set out the psychological conditions that constitute a conceptualization of prejudice that is appropriate for a successful multicultural society that incorporates different ethnic groups:[40]

First, there needs to be general support for multiculturalism, including acceptance of various aspects and consequences of the policy, and of cultural diversity as a valuable resource for a society. Second, there should be overall low levels of intolerance or prejudice in the population. Third, there should be generally positive mutual attitudes among the various ethno-cultural groups that constitute the society. Fourth, there needs to be a degree of attachment to the larger Canadian society, but without derogation of its constituent ethno-cultural groups.

In contrast to these elements is the construct of ethnocentrism, which provides a challenge to multiculturalism. Ethnocentrism theory began with an initial insight of Sumner that in most inter-group situations "one's own group is the center of everything, and all others are scaled and rated with reference to it."[41] He made a basic distinction between the "in" group – the group(s) to which one belongs – and the "out" group (all other groups), and proposed that one's "in" group is usually evaluated more positively than "out" groups. This ethnocentric tendency for in-group favoritism has been identified in many societies, leading Levine and Campbell[42] to claim that it is a universal feature of inter-group relations. The concept of ethnocentrism has also been used as a synonym for general antipathy toward all out groups. For example, the ethnocentrism scale of Adorno et al.[43] has served as a general measure of intolerance for those who differ from oneself, and even as a rejection of diversity as a whole.

Ethnocentrism theory has been employed at both the group and individual levels of analysis. Collectively, groups may exhibit relative preferences with respect to others (e.g., in immigration policy, or social discrimination practices), while individuals within groups can vary widely in their degree of intolerance and in-group/out-group favoritism. This distinction between group and individual levels has been central to most explanations of prejudice, and both are considered essential for a complete theory of inter-group relations.[44]

In his investigation of multiculturalism in Australia, Robert Ho[45] concluded that ethnocentrism correlates negatively with the following dimensions:

1. First, the belief that multiculturalism, as a policy to deal with the country's cultural diversity, is in line with Australia's national interest.
2. Multiculturalism, as a policy to deal with cultural diversity, has benefited Australian society, both culturally and economically..
3. Multiculturalism has enabled ethnic minorities greater access to power resources such as status, wealth, education, government positions and political office.
4. As a social policy, its goal is to ensure that the social cohesion of the nation is preserved – not inter-group conflict.

The objective of this chapter was to provide theoretical support for the establishment of the various dimensions of the study, which is the foucs of chapter 6.

Notes

1. J. Dovidio and V. M. Esses, "Immigrants and Immigration: Advancing the psychological perspective," *Journal of Social Issues* 57(3) (Fall 2001), pp. 375–88.
2. G. J. Borjas, *Heaven's Door: Immigration policy and the American economy* (Princeton, NJ: Princeton University Press, 1999); R. Cohen and Z. Layton-Henry (eds.), *The Politics of Migration* (Northampton, MA: Elgar, 1997); C. Hirschman, P. Kasinitz, and J. DeWind (eds.), *The Handbook of International Migration: The American experience* (New York: Russell Sage Foundation, 1999); R. G. Rumbaut, N. Foner, and S. J. Gold, "Transformations: Introduction. Immigration and immigration research in the United States," *American Behavioral Scientist* 42 (1999), pp. 1258–63.
3. S. Castles, "Migrants and Minorities in Europe: Perspectives for the 1990s: Eleven hypotheses," in J. Solomos and J. Wrench (eds.), *Racism and Migration in Western Europe* (Oxford: Berg, 1993), pp. 17–34.
4. T. F. Pettigrew, "Reactions toward the New Minorities of Western Europe," *Annual Review of Sociology* 24(1) (1998), p. 77.
5. F. Solomos, and J. Wrench, "Race and Racism in Contemporary Europe," in J. Solomos and J. Wrench (eds.), *Racism and Migration in Western Europe* (Oxford: Berg, 1993), pp. 3–16.
6. Borjas, *Heaven's Door*, 1999.
7. R. Cohen and Z. Layton-Henry (eds.), *The Politics of Migration* (Northampton, MA: Elgar, 1997).
8. V. M. Esses, L. M. Jackson, and T. L. Armstrong, "Intergroup Competition and Attitudes Toward Immigrants and Immigration: An instrumental model of group conflict," *Journal of Social Issues* 54(4) (1998), pp. 724–99.
9. M. MacEwen, *Tackling Racism in Europe: An examination of anti-discrimination law in practice* (Washington, D.C.: Berg, 1995).
10. G. W. Allport, *The Nature of Prejudice* (Cambridge, MA: Addison Wesley, 1994), p. 51.
11. Pettigrew, "Reactions toward the New Minorities," p. 79.
12. S. L. Gaertner, M. C. Rust, J. F. Dovidio, B. A. Bachman and P. A. Anastasio, "The Contact Hypothesis: The role of a common in-group identity on reducing inter-group bias among majority and minority group members," in J. L. Nye and A. M. Brower (eds.), *What's Social about Social Cognition?* (Newbury Park, CA: Sage, 1996), pp. 230–360.
13. T. F. Pettigrew and R. W. Meertens, "Subtle and Blatant Prejudice in Western Europe," *European Journal of Social Psychology* 25 (1995), pp. 57–76.
14. C. Wilpert, "Ideological and Institutional Foundations of Racism in the Federal Republic of Germany," in Solomos and Wrench (eds.), *Racism and Migration in Western Europe* (Oxford: Berg, 1993), pp. 67–81.
15. S. Castles, *Here for Good: Western Europe's new ethnic minorities* (London: Pluto, 1984).
16. Wilpert, "Ideological and Institutional Foundations of Racism," p. 70.
17. Ethnic Germans from the former Soviet Union and other Eastern European countries, who automatically receive German citizenship and thus carry

German passports – but who frequently lack German language skills.
18 A. Adelson and Leslie, "Opposing Oppositions: Turkish–German Questions in Contemporary German Studies," *German Studies Review* 17(2) (1994), pp. 304, 305–30.
19 Sigrid Weigel, "Literature der Fremde – Literature in der Fremde," in Klaus Briegleb and Sigrid Weigel (eds.), *Gegenwartsliteratur seit 1968* (München and Wien: Carl Hanser Verlag. Hansers Sozialgeschichte der deutschen Literatur vom 16. Jahrhundert bis zur Gegenwart 12, 1996), pp. 212–13.
20 Sabine Von Dirke, "Multikulti: The German Debate on Multiculturalism," *German Studies Review* 17(3) (1994), pp. 513–36.
21 T. Faist, "How to Define a Foreigner? The symbolic politics of immigration in German partisan discourse, 1978–1992," in M. Baldwin-Edwards, and M. A. Schain (eds.), *The Politics of Immigration in Western Europe* (London: Frank Cass, 1994), pp. 50–71.
22 T. Faist, "Immigration, Integration, and the Welfare State: Germany and USA in a comparative perspective," in R. Baubock, A. Heller and A.R. Zolberg (eds.), *The Challenge of Diversity* (Aldershot: Avebury, 1996), pp. 227–58.
23 Ayse S. Caglar, "Constraining Metaphors and the Transnationalisation of Spaces in Berlin," *Journal of Ethnic and Migration Studies* 27(4) (October 2001), pp. 601–14.
24 Ibid.
25 L. H. Malkki, "National Geographic: The rooting of peoples and the territorialization of national identity among scholars and refugees," *Cultural Anthropology* 7(1) (1992): 24–44.
26 A. Portes and J. Curtis, "Changing Flags: Naturalization and its determinants among Mexican Americans," *International Migration Review* 21 (1987), pp. 352–71.
27 Philip Q. Yang, "Explaining Immigrant Naturalization," *International Migration Review* 28(3) (Fall 1994), pp. 449–78.
28 R. Levine and D. T. Campbell, *Ethnocentrism: Theories of conflict, attitudes and group behavior* (New York: Wiley, 1972); M. W. Giles and A. Evans, "The Power Approach to Intergroup Hostility," *Journal of Conflict Resolution* 30 (1986), pp. 469–86.
29 N. Tienhaara, *Canadian Views on Immigration and Population* (Ottawa: Information Canada, 1974).
30 W. G. Stephan, O. Ybbara, C. Martinez, J. Schwarzwald and M. Tur-Kaspa, "Prejudice toward Immigrants to Spain and Israel: An integrated threat theory analysis," *Journal of Cross-Cultural Psychology* 29 (1998), pp. 559–76.
31 L. Quillian, "Prejudice as a Response to Perceived Group Threat: Population composition and anti-immigrant and racial prejudice in Europe," *American Sociological Review* 60 (1995), pp. 586–611.
32 Douglas Palmer, "Determinants of Canadian Attitudes toward Immigration: More than just racism?" *Canadian Journal of Behavioral Science* 28(3) (1996), pp. 180–92.
33 G. W. Allport, *The Nature of Prejudice* (Cambridge MA: Addison-Wesley, 1954); Y. Amir, "Contact Hypothesis in Ethnic Relations," *Psychological*

Bulletin 71 (1969), pp. 319–41; S.W. Cook, "Experimenting on Social Issues," *American Psychologist* 40 (1985), pp. 452–60; M. Hewstone and R. Brown, *Contact and Conflict in Iintergroup Encounters* (Oxford: Basil Blackwell, 1986).

34 R. B. Zajonc, "Attitudinal Effects of Mere Exposure," *Journal of Personality and Social Psychology* Monograph 9 (2, Part 2) (1968), pp. 1–28.

35 R. M. Williams, *Strangers Next Door: Ethnic relations in American Communities* (Englewood Cliffs, NJ: Prentice-Hall, 1964); R. F. Hamilton, *Class and Politics in the United States* (Toronto: John Wiley and Sons, 1972); W. S. Ford, "Interracial Public Housing in a Border City: Another look at the contact hypothesis," *American Journal of Sociology* 78 (1973), pp. 1426–47.

36 C. Reich. and M. Purbhoo, "The Effect of Cross-Cultural Contact," *Canadian Journal of Behavioral Science* 7 (1975),pp. 313–27.

37 S. Ziegler, "Measuring Inter-Ethnic Attitudes in a Multi-Ethnic Context," *Canadian Ethnic Studies* 12 (1980), pp. 45–55.

38 D. M. George and R. A. Hoppe, "Racial Identification, Preference and Self-Concept," *Journal of Cross-Cultural Psychology* 10 (1979), pp. 85–100.

39 R. Kalin and J. W. Berry, "The Social Ecology of Ethnic Attitudes in Canada," *Canadian Journal of Behavioral Science* 14 (1982), pp. 97–109.

40 J. W. Berry and R. Kalin, "Multicultural and Ethnic Attitudes in Canada: An overview of the 1991 national survey," *Canadian Journal of Behavioral Science* 27 (1995), pp. 301–20.

41 W. G. Sumner, *Folkways* (New York: Ginn, 1906), pp. 27–8.

42 Ibid.

43 T. Adorno, E. Frenkel-Brunswick, D.Levinson and N. Sanford, *The Authoritarian Personality* (New York: Harper, 1950).

44 J. Duckitt, *The Social Psychology of Prejudice* (New York: Praeger, 1992).

45 Robert Ho, "Multiculturalism in Australia: A survey of attitudes," *Human Relations* 43(3) (1990), p. 269.

6
The Research Method

In the conclusion to Part I the normative aspects of Palestinian presence in Lebanon were classified into broad headings. They covered some important issues related to official policies toward Palestinians, and emphasized the interplay between the attitudes held by the various Lebanese communal groups toward Lebanon's Palestinian community and toward the prospects of their permanent settlement in the country. Religious differences seemed to play the major part in forming basic and political attitudes toward Palestinian presence.

In the remainder of this book, the themes provided on attitudes toward Palestinians will be examined empirically, in correspondence with the pertinent theoretical underpinnings.

Despite the limitations of the sample used in the present study, this investigation addresses an important current issue and draws into question some common conceptions about popular attitudes toward Palestinian permanent settlement in Lebanon. The findings are generalizable and may contribute to the larger debate on Palestinian refugees, which has implications for the Lebanese system as a whole.

The objective is to test the components of relevance to Palestinian presence in Lebanon. It is well known that increased interaction and contact with a certain group influences interethnic acceptance of members of this group and decreases out-group animosity. Consequently, positive affect derived from inter-group contact may well override cognitive barriers to broader socio-political issues, and may serve to attenuate tension and generate empathy.

Therefore, the following nine variables will be used to measure socio-political attitudes toward Palestinians, out of which hypotheses will be generated:

1. Lebanese blame Palestinians for the early years (1975–6) of the civil war.
2. Lebanese display hostility toward the Palestinians.
3. Lebanese do not empathize with the Palestinians.
4. Lebanese interact rarely with Palestinians.

5. Lebanese tend to discriminate against Palestinians (anti-Palestinianism).
6. Lebanese are aware of resettlement projects.
7. Lebanese are likely to reject an imposed resettlement.
8. Lebanese perceive the impact of resettlement negatively.
9. Lebanese are going to resist the implementation of resettlement.

Operational and Field Measures

The survey instrument

A total of 42 items were used in the Lebanese questionnaire. In developing the survey instrument, an initial pool of items was constructed from two sources. Approximately half of the items were adapted from existing instruments.[1] The remaining items were developed anew by the investigator. Many of the items adapted from previous instruments were reworded to simplify their readability. English- and Arabic-language versions of the questionnaires were prepared. A copy of the interview schedule is available from the author.

Sources of the data

The study was based on a quota sample of 1,073 Lebanese respondents, and was carried out in late December 1999 and January 2000, using a face-to-face interviewing procedure. The response rate, based upon the number of completed interviews as compared with those attempted, was 80%. In practice, not all selected people were interviewed. Some refused and others completed only part of the questionnaire.

The sample included five occupational sub-groups, selected on the basis of quota sampling necessitated by the fact that representative selection is not possible due to lack of accurate demographic data pertaining to the characteristics and the urban distribution of the population. Because the sample is non-probabilistic, it is important to describe its characteristics and to note that, in some respects, they differ from those of the larger Lebanese population over the age of 18. The sex distribution of the sample consisted of 64% male and 36% female. The lower proportion of women in the study reflects their marginal position in Lebanese society dominated by males, as well as their limited professional role.

The age distribution of the respondents included 40% in the category of 18–25 years, 32% in the category of 26–35 years, 18% in the category 36–45 years and 11% in the category 46 years and older. The representation of each confessional group is, as close as possible (noting that there has been no official census since 1932) in proportion to its actual size in Lebanon's population: 29% Maronite, 10% Greek-Catholic, 9% Greek-Orthodox, 27% Shi'ite, 18% Sunni and 7% Druze. In terms of educational level, the sample was found to be over-represented in the college-educated level, with 58% having achieved college education.

In terms of occupational groupings, the sample somewhat over-represented people with professional and managerial occupations, and under-represented people in the trades and labor category.[2]

Quality of the data

Despite some limitations, including the non-representative composition and the relatively small size of the sample, this data constitutes an empirical foundation possessing considerable strength: First, the availability of opinion data dealing with socio-political issues is itself a notable strength because surveys dealing with political attitudes are extremely rare in the Arab world. In fact, Lebanon is the only Arab country where public opinion polls regarding political issues are conducted without official interference; this further enhances the reliability of the findings.[3] In addition, the Lebanese are considered to be a politically knowledgeable people, thanks to their blatant exposure to political information and the continued existence of independent medias and free press in the country.

Second, the respondents were interviewed in an atmosphere of strict confidentiality, and well-trained interviewers of the same religious background interviewed the respondents in their native language, Arabic. Moreover, the interviewers participating in this study were informed on the topic. They were fully instructed by the author on the techniques of sample selection. The questionnaire was fully discussed with them; they became familiar with each item, and by the time they went in to the field they were in a position to interpret to their respondents any questionnaire-related ambiguities. Equally important, they were trained to be objective during the administration of the questions and not to attempt to influence the responses.

The initial responses conveyed by the respondents to their interviewers were almost always apprehensive and discouraging. However, once the researchers explained the objectives of the study, and as soon as their status was recognized by their respondents, interviewer–respondent relationships became congenial. The survey was eventually concluded after an adequate number of questionnaires had been completed. The author also maintained close contact with the field workers during the entire period of data collection and personally supervised the stage of data-processing (coding and entry), including tabular preparation and presentation.

Third, a pre-test was administered to 40 respondents of varying age and

The Research Method

occupation. As a result of respondents' comments, some of the questions were rewritten in a clear and direct form in the final format of the questionnaire and some were deleted.

In order to avoid random error, the researcher tried to shorten the period of administration of the questionnaire, which did not exceed fifty days. This was intended to avoid sudden political changes. The respondents themselves represented the researcher with significant clues for the evaluation of the quality of their responses. Any knowledgeable observer can immediately discern the consistency and pattern of reality of the sample. But in general, respondents attested that the questions were interesting and well understood.

Furthermore, the initial questionnaire was translated into Arabic by the researcher himself and, as a check on the accuracy of the translation, two Arabic-speaking qualified persons retranslated the questionnaire into English. Discrepancies between the original English version and the retranslated version were then discussed and resolved. However, in general, respondents attested that the questions were easily understood. In order to achieve a great measure of questionnaire reliability, the author ensured that:

1. The questionnaire had a central topic; it emphasized attitudes toward the Palestinian community in Lebanon and the prospect of their permanent settlement in the country. The objectives were unambiguously stated in an attached letter of appreciation.
2. The questionnaire sought only information that cannot be obtained from non-survey data.
3. The questionnaire requested essential data; the questions were as concise as possible.
4. Respondents were given clear and complete instructions on how to answer each item. Furthermore, each question dealt with only one idea.
5. The questions were objectively constructed with no hint for desired responses.
6 Questions were presented in good psychological order, proceeding from general to more specific responses.

Given the precarious nature of survey research in a conflicted environment, four reliability test measures were also imposed on the data: internal consistency, response bias, congruence with reality and analysis of the variance.

The test for internal consistency compared the percentage distributions of several pairs of several items. In this regard, 86% of those respondents who claimed to belong to the upper class also stated that their income was average or above average. Examination of middle-class respondents showed that 76% were of average income while 20% reported a below-average income. Among the working-class respondents, 56% reported an average income, while the 38% reported that their income was below average.

For the problem of response bias, three sets of similar items, presented in reverse order, were examined to determine if any tendency occurred for respondents to answer either first or last responses with greater frequencies. No such tendency occurred.

Third, as to congruence with reality, response patterns derived from the survey were evaluated by a panel of experts, and the results were found to be consistent and congruent with the context of the study by all members of the panel.

Fourth, as the survey was conducted by several interviewers, it was deemed advisable to test for reliability of the sub-populations. The one-way analysis of variance test (ANOVA) was applied to the sub-samples and no significant difference emerged between response patterns of the sub-samples.

The validity of the instrument was ensured based on panel discussions, and theoretical support for all the research variables was obtained from the pertinent literature. Wherever applicable, factor analysis was used to verify the unidimensionality of the scales. A summary of all items to generate the scales used in the study, and the factor analysis procedures, are shown in the appendix.

An additional word on the Palestinian sample

The Palestinian data rests on a simple random sample of 273 respondents interviewed at and outside the camps for Palestinian refugees.[4] The data was collected during the months of July and August 2002.

Field researchers in the camps were confronted with several problems. First, the association of interviewers with mischievous domestic and foreign agencies was a problem, which the researcher and his interviewers were aware of. However, the greatest problems that stood in the face of questionnaire administration in the camps were security related. The survey took place at a moment of intense instability in Palestinian politics, in particular at the Ain al-Hilweh camp in south Lebanon near Sidon. Out of the 12 Palestinian camps in Lebanon, this camp remains under direct and almost full control of the PLO, with a token presence of Islamic fundamentalist groups such as Osbat al-Ansar and the Dinnieh group. During the summer of 2002, recurring clashes occurred between the Lebanese Army and Muslim fanatics based in the camp at an initial stage, and later on between PLO fighters and Islamists.[5]

Despite the non-inclusion of off-camp refugees and limiting the data to

The Research Method

Palestinian camp refugees, the data possess considerable strength and allows for generalizations. Conditions of life in all refugee camps are invariably the same: dismal. The camps, which provide nearly all recruits for the plethora of Palestine movements, have also been a hotbed of radicalism and the staging ground for terrorist attacks. Furthermore, the camps serve as a poignant reminder that the Palestinian refugee problem has not yet been solved.

With the parameters of the study established, we may now undertake an analysis of the responses, starting with political orientations toward Palestinians.

Notes

1. G. W. Allport, *The Nature of Prejudice* (Cambridge, MA: Addison Wesley, 1954); Hilal Khashan, "Palestinian Resettlement in Lebanon: Behind the Debate," *Montreal Studies on the contemporary Arab World* (April 1994); Giuseppe Labianca, Daniel Brass and Barbara Gray, "Social Networks and Perceptions of Intergroup Conflict: The role of negative relationships and third parties," *Academy of Management Journal* 41(1) (1998), pp. 55–68; Stephen Tuch, Lee Sigleman and Jason Macdonald, "The Polls – Trends: Race relations and American youth, 1976–1995," *Public Opinion Quarterly* 63(11) (1999), pp. 109–14; Ann Bettancourt, and Nancy Dorr, "Cooperative Interaction and Intergroup Bias: Effects of numerical representation and crosscut role assignment," *Personality and Social Psychology Bulletin* 24(12) 1998, pp. 1276–98.

2. The author sought to broaden the representativeness of the sample by including 20 professions which were regrouped into five sub-groups for reasons of data manageability: 19% professionals, 40% semi-professionals, 11% unskilled, 25% college students (selected from three private academic institutions: Notre Dame University and Lebanese University, and the American University of Beirut), and 5% unemployed.

3. A survey of attitudes on opinion polls in Lebanon, by Information International, revealed that 93 percent of the people who have been interviewed said they conveyed always-correct responses to their interviewers, *An-Nahar*, Beirut, May 5, 2002.

4. The number of refugees registered with UNRWA as of March 31, 1999 was 368,527, of whom 201,226 (54.6%) lived in camps. Nonetheless, the researcher was told that the real number did not exceed 130,000.

5. During the summer of 2002, factional conflict inside Lebanon's largest Palestinian refugee camp erupted between the mainstream Fatah group and radical Islamist groups. The conflict centers on members of a Lebanese Sunni fundamentalist group accused of links to the al-Qaeda terror network who took refuge in Ain el-Helweh after being defeated by the Lebanese army in clashes in northern Lebanon in January 2000. In July 2002, a Lebanese Islamist who had been holed up in Ain el-Helweh after killing three Lebanese military

intelligence officers was surrendered when Osbat al-Ansar intervened, under pressure from the Palestinian Islamic Resistance Movement, a splinter group from the fundamentalist Osbat al-Ansar, known by its acronym Hamas and which is on the US list of suspected terrorist organisations. On August 13, 2002 a member of Fatah and a fundamentalist were killed and eight other people wounded in a clash, after Jamat al-Nur threatened to cause a "bloodbath" if the fugitives were handed over to the Lebanese army.

7

Basic Political Views of Palestinians

The purpose of this chapter is to test the veracity of the conventional wisdom hypotheses, established in chapter 3. The scope of these hypotheses range from group perception and blame for war to empathy with Palestinians and their nationalistic cause. Survey analysis was utilized to measure the following variables:

1. Lebanese blame the civil war on Palestinians.
2. Lebanese do not empathize with Palestinians.
3. Lebanese are hostile to Palestinians.

Levels of Hostility and Empathy toward Palestinians

Conventional wisdom stresses Lebanese Sunni and Palestinian solidarity. This is contrasted by Lebanese Christian and Shi'ite distaste for Palestinians. Therefore, there is every reason to assume that Christians and Shi'ites would blame Palestinians for the Lebanese civil war, and also to display hostility against them. By the same reasoning, one should encounter little, if any, hostility by the Sunnis against Palestinians.

How did respondents perceive Palestinians? The thermometer scale[1] was used as an accurate measure of Lebanese respondents' feelings toward Palestinians. The results are shown in table 7.1, which measures the level of warmth or hostility toward Palestinians. The percentages indicate in striking fashion that Lebanese groups display little warmth toward Palestinians (22%), whereas 58 percent do not favor them. Another 21 percent of respondents showed mixed feelings. An exception were Sunni and Druze respondents' scores.

Communal tensions were already endemic in Lebanon when many displaced Palestinians entered the country in 1948. Political scientist Farid al-Khazen remarks that:

> Palestinians came to Lebanon at a time when differences within Lebanese society had reached a considerable degree of political maturity and when the

Basic Political Views of Palestinians

confessional structure of Lebanese society had taken its present shape. In other words, there was little room for newcomers to Lebanon's communal and political landscape . . . they had to carve out a place of their own, but only at the expense of existing communal and political structures.[2]

Originally, the Palestinians were not the source of conflict. They became a disruptive political issue in Lebanese politics only after 1969. That year heralded the beginning of Palestinian use of military bases in south Lebanon to wage their raids against Israeli settlements in the upper Galilee.

Table 7.1 Relations between religious background and communal closeness/hostility to Palestinians (N=716)

	Maronites N=218	G-C N=67	G-O N=75	Sunnis N=113	Shi'ites N=184	Druze N=59
Close	9	10	13	44	23	44
Neutral	17	12	24	24	22	29
Distant	74	78	63	32	55	27

Cramer's V = 0.28
Alpha = 0.05

Notes: Here, and in all tables, "N" represents the number of respondents; figures are in percentages; and columns may not add up to 100 because results were rounded to the nearest whole number.

G-C stands for Greek-Catholics; G-O stands for Greek-Orthodox.

In most tables, the Cramer V value establishes a meaningful association between the independent variable ("religious affiliation") and the dependent variable (the question), permitting a breakdown by religious affiliation. In others that lack this statistically meaningful association, the breakdown by religious affiliation is provided for comparison.

Based on the historical relations between Palestinians and Sunnis, it is unlikely that the Sunnis would project hostility against Palestinians for the following reasons: First, the majority of Palestinians are Sunni Muslims. In a country fraught with age-old confessional disputes, this confessional bond is expected to foster fraternal links between the two groups. Sunnis' moderate hostility toward Palestinians should be reinforced by the massive military support the latter gave the former throughout the civil war.

On another level, Palestinian displacement and loss of identity in 1948 relegated them to a secondary status by their Lebanese Sunnis co-religionists. The exclusion of Palestinians from governmental positions and business circles, their inability to obtain decent employment in the country, and the reliance of a substantial number of them on foreign agencies and

Basic Political Views of Palestinians

the United Nations for economic and educational aid, contributed to their negative perception by the Sunnis.

On the other hand, most Christians have always been hostile to the Palestinians, due mainly to Palestinian exploitation of the internal tensions of Lebanese society for their own ends. To the Maronites, "Palestinian refugees are the source of our calamities . . . They have pushed Christian–Muslim contradictions to the front – i.e., toward the 'Islamization' of Lebanon, a country whose culture is humanistic and whose faith is Christian."[3]

In fact, Maronites' extreme fear of the Palestinian element is due to the fact that the vast majority of Palestinians are Sunni Muslims. The Maronites view them as a major destabilizing force capable of upsetting the country's precarious sectarian balance, on whose basis Maronite supremacy was founded. It became imperative that the Maronites oppose the rising militancy of the Palestinians, especially after the 1967 Six Day War, at any cost, even if it meant civil war.

While the Maronites are concerned about the potential damage Palestinian presence in Lebanon can do to their community, the Shi'ites in south Lebanon have borne the brunt of fierce and heavy-handed Israeli retaliation for Palestinian guerilla raids against Israeli targets. The rise of Palestinian militarism sped up the process of Shi'ite mobilization and anti-Palestinian sentiment among the Shi'ite rank-and-file. It is often asserted that hatred for the Palestinians was one of the very few issues that the Syrian-backed Shi'ite Amal Movement and the Maronites had in common.

The intensity of Palestinian–Shi'ite rivalry was clearly demonstrated by the War of the Camps. This war had devastating results for the Palestinians. It was carried out by Syria and the Shi'ite Amal militia to ensure a dispersal of the Palestinian refugees. Thus its goal was the destruction of the camps and such a diminution of Palestinian numbers that they would never regain political power or autonomy in Lebanon.[4] In 1990, Palestinian military expansion in Iklim al-Tufah, a region in the south, led to bloody encounters between Palestinians and the Shi'ite Hizbullah.

The Sunnis are expected to project less hostility toward Palestinians than other communal groups. This lack of hostility is reinforced by the fact that both groups were allies during the civil war, with Palestinians acting as the "sword" of the Sunnis.

During the 1960s and 1970s, Lebanese Sunnis regarded the military presence of the PLO in Lebanon as a "historical opportunity to restore the justice, the anomaly that constitutes Lebanon in the heart of an Arab world, where Christians participate greatly in power."[5] Consequently, the Sunnis perceived the PLO as a Sunni Muslim army. The broad Sunni support for the Palestinians grew as much out of a desire to weaken an

Basic Political Views of Palestinians

opposing power (the Maronite-dominated establishment) as it did out of Arab and Islamic solidarity.

Lebanon's civil war, which undermined the traditional Sunni elite, also created a power vacuum among the Muslims. During the rise of PLO power in Lebanon in the 1970s, most Lebanese Sunnis, begrudging the preponderance of Maronite power, found in the Palestinian military machine a consolation for their political inefficacy, and hoped that they might deploy it to reverse what they considered an inequitable status quo. For the Sunnis, therefore, the PLO was regarded as a legitimate organization with whom they could easily identify.

As a small religious group, Lebanese Druze began to confront a new political reality after the onset of the civil war, when firepower turned into a new source of political expression. As the new rules of the political game necessitated militia power, in which the Druze were deficient, they found in the forces of the PLO a rare substitute which allowed them to remain a potent actor in Lebanese politics. The importance of the Palestinian connection was indisputably recognized by most Druze respondents. After all, the Druze needed practical allies, and these proved to be the Palestinians.

Table 7.2 Relationship between religious background and blaming Palestinians for civil war (N=1034)

	Maronites N=302	G-C N=108	G-O N=94	Sunnis N=182	Shi'ites N=276	Druze N=72
Yes	93	93	96	75	89	61
No	7	7	4	25	11	39
Unsure	—	—	—	—	—	—

Cramer's V = 0.29
Alpha = 0.05

Table 7.3 Relationship between religious background and group responsibility for civil war (N=1003)

	Maronites N=296	G-C N=103	G-O N=9	Sunnis N=173	Shi'ites N=269	Druze N=66
Palestinians	46	43	43	15	31	14
All parties	40	40	38	36	28	26
Lebanese parties	14	18	20	50	42	61

Cramer's V = 0.26
Alpha = 0.05

Basic Political Views of Palestinians

As shown in table 7.2, Lebanese respondents are quick to point fingers to Palestinian responsibility for the devastating civil war. Nonetheless, they are ready to concede the responsibility of Lebanese parties. In response to an item concerning group responsibility for the civil war, the data showed that 34 percent of the respondents blamed the war solely on the Palestinians, whereas 31 percent blamed it on Lebanese groups. Another 33 percent felt all groups equally responsible for the war (see table 7.3).

The date generally given for the start of the civil war in Lebanon is April 13, 1975, the day unidentified assailants reportedly shot a member of the Kataeb, or Phalange Party, in front of a church, and right-wing Christian gunmen retaliated by ambushing a bus full of Palestinians in a Christian sector of Beirut. Many Lebanese blame the Palestinians for providing the fuel for the civil war that laid waste to their country from 1975 to 1990. And while they are reluctant to recall the murderous fighting that went on between Lebanese militias, they are quick to point fingers at the Palestinians, whose cross-border attacks on northern Israel prompted the Israelis to invade Lebanon in 1982.

The sad truth is that every communal group differs in their perception of the causes and extent of the blame for the civil war and disruption. The civil war was essentially a confrontation between Maronite militiamen and Palestinian guerrillas with whom the Lebanese Muslims soon sided. The Christian right adopted a strategy of defending the Lebanese cause against the Palestinian cause, which they felt must not be fought on Lebanese soil. Therefore, from a Maronite perspective the war was seen as an ideological war fought between Christian militias who defended Lebanon's sovereignty and the Palestinians who encroached upon this sovereignty. By defending the legitimate government, the Christians felt that they were in fact defending the privileged position they occupied in the country, and which constituted the only guarantee for their existence in a hostile environment.

While it is therefore perhaps natural that Christians and Shi'ites would hold Palestinians responsible for the war, such Sunni responses were unexpected. How could the Sunnis possibly incriminate the Palestinians, their allies and arm suppliers, for the conflict? True, the Palestinians openly participated in the fighting, but only at the invitation of the Sunnis. The inability of the Sunnis to cope with the Maronites in the battlefield spurred them to appeal for the PLO for help. Once actively fighting on behalf of the Sunnis, the Palestinians found themselves in a position to extend their control over 80 percent of Lebanon. Thanks to their successful military campaign, the Palestinians emerged as the dominant group in the leftist camp. The Palestinians' rise to power had antagonized the Sunnis without helping Muslims assert themselves. They do not blame the Palestinians for the civil war, but for its essentially unresolved outcome.

Basic Political Views of Palestinians

Israel's eviction of the PLO in 1982 resulted in a serious decline in Lebanon and facilitated the assertion of Shi'ite power, much of its impetus aimed at replacing the Sunnis in a new political partnership with the Maronites. The Sunnis lag far behind other major Lebanese religious groups in terms of political organization and mass mobilization.

The withdrawal of the PLO resulted in a serious political decline of Sunni influence in the country, the first manifestation being the Sunnis' exclusion from the Tripartite Agreement of 1985. As for the Druze, in 1976 their leader Kamal Jumblatt felt that the PLO's military presence in Lebanon offered the Druze a rare opportunity to extract political concessions from the Maronite ruling class. Military and political alliances between Druze and Palestinian leadership facilitated closer ties between the Druze and Palestinian communities. On the other hand, the Druze standpoint in the poll probably also has to do with the outcome of the 1983 Mountain War, when the Druze alliance with Palestinian factions proved to be the turning point for the former's victory over the right-wing Lebanese Forces militia.

Table 7.4 Relationship between religious background and extent of Palestinian responsibility for war in Lebanon (N=1026)

	Maronites N=297	G-C N=106	G-O N=98	Sunnis N=182	Shi'ites N=274	Druze N=69
To a great extent	50	48	45	20	38	23
To a certain extent	42	41	41	43	46	44
Not at all	8	11	14	37	16	33

Cramer's V = 0.22
Alpha = 0.05

Table 7.5 Relationship between religious background and empathizing with Palestinians (N=1,057

	Maronites N=306	G-C N=107	G-O N=101	Sunnis N=191	Shi'ites N=280	Druze N=72
Most of the time	10	13	8	40	30	38
Sometimes	26	41	34	39	44	44
Never	65	46	58	22	26	1

Cramer's V = 0.3
Alpha = 0.05

Emotional empathy has often been labeled as sympathy, affective empathy, affective perspective taking, or emotional responsiveness.[6] Empathy refers primarily to emotional responses to another person (member of an ethnic out-group) that either are similar to those the other person is experiencing (parallel empathy) or are a reaction to the emotional experiences of the other person (reactive empathy). If one sympathizes with another person's pain and discomfort, one is experiencing reactive empathy (one's emotional reaction to the other's situation), whereas if one responds with feelings of indignation and resentment toward the person, one is more likely experiencing parallel empathy (feeling emotions similar to those of the out-group member). Batson, Polycarpou et al. argue that there is an attitude change in response to reactive empathy,[7] particularly because concern for the welfare of this person generalizes to the group of which this person is a member, leading to more "positive beliefs about, feelings toward, and concern for the group." Finlay and Stephan[8] suggest that parallel empathy leads to attitude change by arousing feelings of injustice. Learning about suffering and discrimination while empathizing with the victims may lead people to reappraise their assumptions concerning victim blame, and they may come to believe that the victims do not deserve the mistreatment to which they are being subjected. If the victims do not deserve this unjust treatment, it may no longer be tenable to hold such negative attitudes toward them.

Table 7.4 attests that Muslim respondents showed more sympathy toward Palestinians than their Christian counterparts. Next, tables 7.5 and 7.6 demonstrate how the continued existence of the refugee problem symbolizes for the Palestinians the nature of their plight and the historical injustice done to them. Lebanese respondents' acknowledgment of the righteousness of the refugees' political and moral cause to Israel proper is at the heart of the justice of the Palestinian cause. The essence of the refugee issue is more than a matter of living conditions, residency rights or resettlement in and absorption by host countries. Also, it is not a humanitarian issue alone; rather, first and foremost, it is a political issue.

Other reasons were war-related: During the civil war, Palestinian refugees were themselves often targets of violence. First, they were attacked by right-wing Christian militias – slaughtered in Tal al-Zaatar in 1976 and in the Sabra and Shatila refugee camps in 1982. Later on came the devastating War of the Camps, initiated by the Syrian-backed Shi'ite Amal militia.

The third reason was humanitarian: Lebanon is the only host country where the quota of camp inhabitants who are still refugees is still higher than 50 percent of the total number of refugees in that country, and they suffer as a result of their miserable conditions.[9]

One should not forget that the Shi'ites espoused the Palestinian cause during the early stages of the war because of their own sense of relative deprivation. Despite the manifest hatred displayed by Amal militiamen against Palestinian refugees during the War of the Camps, the effects of this

Basic Political Views of Palestinians

war are revealing: Not only did Hizbullah – the Party of God – side with the Palestinians in the conflict, but leading Shi'ite clerics also condemned the attacks. As an act of protest by the rank-and-file, a great number of Amal members also left the movement.[10]

On the other hand, the position of Lebanese Christians is summarized by Pierre Gemayel's letter to Henry Kissinger:[11] "The Lebanese Christians recognize Palestinian rights in their homeland . . . and support the establishment of a dual homeland for the Jews and Palestinians . . . Israel continues to be rejected in the Arab region."

According to Abu Khalil,[12] this position of sympathy changed only when Palestinians started to violate all agreements with the Lebanese state.

Table 7.6 Relationship between religious background and instances where you have empathized with Palestinians (N=412)

	Maronites N=75	G-C N=36	G-O N=29	Sunnis N=95	Shi'ites N=147	Druze N=30
Because they were abandoned by the international community	32	42	41	37	35	13
Because they were targets for violence	23	31	24	30	36	67
Because of their adverse social and economic conditions	45	28	35	28	29	20

Cramer's V = 0.18
Alpha = 0.05

Notes

1   The operationalization of communal closeness or hostility was based on one item requesting respondents to list how close they felt (closest, second closest, neutral, second least close, least close) to Palestinians. This procedure clearly reflected the use of a thermometer to indicate party or ideological preference in Western voting studies. The responses thus acquired were recorded to provide interval closeness versus hostility scale for the Palestinians. In somewhat simplified terms, the scaling procedure involved assigning each sect two points for each closest response, one point for each second closest response, zero points for neutral or not mentioned response, minus one point for each second least close response, and minus two points for each least close response.
2   Farid El-Khazen, *The Breakdown of The State in Lebanon* (London and New York: I. B. Tauris Publishers, 2000), p. 132.
3   M. Zuaytir, *Al-Mashruu al-Maruni fi Lubnan* (The Maronite Project in Lebanon), (Beirut: Wikalat al-Tawzii al-Duwaliyya), p. 705.

4   Julie Peteet, "Identity Crisis: Palestinians in post-war Lebanon," *Worldwide Refugee Information* (Washington, D.C.: US Committee for Refugees, 1999), p. 3.
5   See Annie Laurent and Antoine Basbous, *Guerres Secrètes au Liban* (Paris, Gallimard, 1987), p. 40. Having lacked both the motive and the opportunity to develop a competitive politico-military apparatus similar to other confessional groups, Lebanese had to identify with the PLO to press their political demands on the Lebanese establishment.
6   Walter G. Stephan and Krystina Finlay, "The Role of Empathy in Improving Inter-group Relations." *Journal of Social Issues* 55(4) (Winter 1999), p. 729.
7   C. D. Batson, M. P. Polycarpou, E. Harmon-Jones, H. J. Imhoff, E. C. Mitchener, L. L Bednar, T. R. Klein and L. Highberger, "Empathy and Attitudes: Can feeling for a member of a stigmatized group improve feelings toward the group?," *Journal of Personality and Social Psychology* 72 (1997), pp. 105–118.
8   K. A. Finlay and W. G. Stephan, "Reducing Prejudice: The effects of empathy on inter-group attitudes," *Journal of Applied Social Psychology* (in press).
9   Rosemary Sayyigh, "Palestinians in Lebanon: Harsh present, uncertain future," *Journal of Palestine Studie* 25(1) (Autumn 1995), p. 42.
10 Rosemary Sayyigh, *Too Many Enemies*, p. 318.
11 Joseph Abou-Khalil, *Kissat al-Mawarina fi al-Harb: Sirat Zatiat* (The History of the Maronites during the Civil War: A biography), (Beirut, Sharikat al-Matbouat li al-Tawsik wa al-Nashr, 1990), p.16.
12 Ibid., p.17.

8

The Socio-Economic Integration of Palestinians

This chapter explores the different dimensions and practices that facilitate or hamper social and civic integration of Palestinians in a manner that minimizes or increases adverse impact on the Lebanese population and measures the potentials for community tensions. The integration of Palestinians in Lebanon depends in good part on the attitudes of others in that country.

The civil war caused Lebanon incalculable problems, but restoring peace in the country is believed by many to be heavily contingent on the future Palestinian presence. The intensity with which the Lebanese refer to the continued Palestinian presence as the main problem indicates visibility toward this group and provides insights into the nature of communal relations, as well as to the development of group hostility – which contributes to justifying the Lebanese government's reluctance to ease refugee suffering in the camps. The variables examined are: (1) personal contact with Palestinians; (2) communication with Palestinians; (3) tolerance for Palestinians; and (4) position on Palestinian civil rights.

Contact with Palestinians

Table 8.1 Frequency of contact with Palestinians based on religious background (N=1046)

	Maronites N=302	G-C N=106	G-O N=100	Sunnis N=190	Shi'ites N=276	Druze N=72
Yes	20	22	35	60	42	32
No	80	78	65	40	58	68

Cramer's V = 0.30
Alpha = 0.05

The Socio-Economic Integration of Palestinians

Conflict theories argue that frequent and strong relationships among groups increase inter-group cooperation and mitigate inter-group conflict. G. W. Allport stipulates that to increase inter-group acceptance, members of distinct groups (e.g., ethnic groups) should have opportunities to interact with each other.[1] To this end, he specified key structural features that are essential for positive inter-group contact. Among the most important of these features are cooperative interdependence, equal status in the contact setting, interpersonal intimacy and sanction among those in authority. Similarly, numerous studies[2] have shown that cooperation between members of different social groups (frequency of interaction) reduces both biased favoritism toward in-group members and animosity toward out-group members (inter-group conflict). The objective of this measure is to ascertain the type and extent of Lebanese group interaction with Palestinians, and its frequency across groups.

One consequence of the war was the expulsion of those Palestinians who had taken refuge in Christian-controlled areas to other parts of the country. As a result of forced internal migration and also physical immobility, one could expect Palestinian interaction with Sunni and Shi'ite groups exclusively.

Tables 8.1 and 8.2 suggest that personal contacts between respondents and Palestinians are very limited. Two-thirds of respondents disclaimed any relations with Palestinians, while most of those who reported an association spoke only in terms of simple friendship. Other areas of contact included occupational, residential, civic and political contacts, all of which were narrow in scope.

Table 8.2 Relationships between religious background and area of most important personal contact with Palestinians, in percentages

	Maronites N=60	G-C N=23	G-O N=35	Sunnis N=114	Shi'ites N=115	Druze N=14
Friendship	55	52	43	49	51	61
Occupational	5	17	11	12	12	22
Fraternal or civic	12	22	11	11	20	—
Residential	18	9	31	16	20	9
Political	—	—	3	12	12	—

Cramer's V = 0.15
Alpha = 0.05

Religion appears to be related to the magnitude of contact between the respondents and members of Lebanon's Palestinian community. One would expect the Sunnis to interact more often with Palestinians than any other Lebanese group. This assumption rests on the established tendency among the Lebanese to prefer residence near their co-religionists. This tendency was true for the Palestinian refugees who came to Lebanon in 1948: most of them chose to reside inside or near Sunni enclaves. Prior to that, Armenian immigrants who fled Turkish persecution during World War I settled in East Beirut (the Christian half of the capital). As revealed by the findings from this study, Sunni respondents reported frequent contacts with members of the Palestinian community – more than any other Lebanese group, even – but not political relations.

As might be expected, Christian respondents reported infrequent personal contact with Palestinians. Several factors could explain the pattern of responses: First, Palestinian visibility was reduced in post-civil war Lebanon. Refugee camps were scattered among the different Lebanese regions; some, such as Shatila and Bourj al-Brarajneh in Beirut, and Ain al-Hilweh in Sidon, had merged with surrounding Lebanese areas. Today, few Palestinians remain in Christian-dominated areas; rather, they tend to be concentrated in areas of Shi'ite demographic preponderance (the south, Beirut's southern suburbs, the Bekaa Valley). A history of bloodshed reinforces Shi'ite visibility of Palestinians in addition to outright opposition to their presence by mainstream Shi'ite leaders. Second, violent clashes are frequently reported inside Palestinian camps. Probably fear of endangering their own life and property explains the Lebanese respondents' negative stance.

As civil marriages are infrequent, most people are accustomed to marrying within the same religious faith, and probably the same sectarian group. The fact that Armenians are still today not well integrated in Lebanese society enhances this proposition. While differences in faith should be considered part of the reason, for many people a long history of bloodshed between Christians and Palestinians has not yet been overcome.

Communication with Palestinians

The respondents were next asked to indicate the frequency with which they communicated with Palestinians, ranking this on a scale of 1 to 5. The summary communication scale illustrates the conspicuously low levels of Lebanese communications with Palestinians, as evinced in table 8.3. Sunni and Druze respondents seem much more ready to communicate with Palestinians. Actually, the percentages of Lebanese groups' interaction with Palestinians are not impressive: The highest percentage recorded was less than 16% of Druze respondents, indicating a strong interaction pattern, with the Sunnis scoring 33% as opposed to 2%, 5% and 8% for Greek-Orthodox, Greek-Catholics and Maronites, respectively. Realizing that far more Palestinians and Shi'ites reside in and around most refugee camps than Sunnis, the figures for the Muslim groups are hardly surprising.

In absolute numbers the Sunnis do interact more often with other Muslim groups than with non-Muslim groups. Judging from the demographic distribution, this tendency for increased interaction with Palestinians exists in reality.

Table 8.3 Relationship between religious background and intensity of Lebanese groups' communication with Palestinians, in percentages (N=872)

	Maronites N=260	G-C N=87	G-O N=82	Sunnis N=157	Shi'ites N=221	Druze N=65
High	16	25	24	61	48	65
Medium	15	18	13	8	11	6
Low	69	56	62	31	42	29

Cramer's V = 0.27
Alpha = 0.05

As indicated by Barakat, the different confessional groups in Lebanon represent a mosaic of people of infrequent interaction mitigated by religious factors. The history of Lebanon's intercommunal relations is a history characterized by conflict, sectarian independence, low cooperation and minimal social contact. The relations within each sect superseded relations between them. As a result of such low contact, mutual feelings of trust and loyalties are also low. The summary communication scales with Sunnis and Maronites (tables 8.4 and 8.5) illustrate low levels of intergroup communication between Christian and Muslim groups in general. The responses indicate that inter-communal tensions remain perpetuated and accentuated in post-war Lebanon.

Both Catholic and Orthodox respondents indicate the Maronites as the sect with which they are most likely to communicate. Similarly, Shi'ite respondents also report that they communicate slightly more comfortably with the Sunnis but this is not the case for the Druze. Shi'ite worries regarding all other sects, with the exception of the Sunnis, emanate from current Lebanese political environment. The Ta'if Agreement enhanced not only Shi'ite political representation, but also the authority of the Sunni prime minister, from whom they are able to extract political, social and economic demands relative to the pre-war Maronite neglect. All three Muslim groups' level of communication with the Maronites is generally low. The Druze respondents' low propensity for communication with Christians is related to the displacement of Christian residents from Southern Mount Lebanon (Shuff and Aley region) in 1983. The withdrawal of Israel's troops deliberately ignited the War of the Mountains and provoked the forced relocation of the majority of Christians living in the area towards Christian-controlled areas. This war has led to confessional

The Socio-Economic Integration of Palestinians

homogeneity in a previously heterogeneous region.[3] This reality hindered Druze interaction with Christians, namely Maronites, for a relatively long period. In support of this argument, it is important to report that there was a positive relationship between Druze respondents region of residence and communication with all three Christian groups.

Christian respondents report substantially higher percentages of communication with Maronites than the Shi'ites and Druze with Sunnis. However, the intensity of Christian respondents' communication with Sunnis was invariably low. Their attitudes indicate that they have an inherent fear and lack confidence in Muslims. While pre-war Lebanon was established on the basis of cooperation between Christians and Muslims, it seems that the war has rendered communication between different sects harder to achieve. Whether the Maronites, and other Christian communities, can work with Muslim groups to achieve a viable pluralist society is very much in doubt.

Table 8.4 Relationship between religious background and communication with Sunnis, in percentages (N=725)

	Maronites N=248	G-C N=90	G-O N=83	Shi'ites N=239	Druze N=65
High	25	22	22	55	33
Medium	38	44	55	40	56
Low	37	34	23	5	20

Lebanese politics still operates along sectarian lines, and no religious group appears ready to forsake their authority in favor of a more unified system. President Elias Hrawi's proposal to permit civil marriage, and thus weaken the country's sectarian system, created nothing but strife. If one could analyze the mood and concerns of the country's major sects in the post-Ta'if period, one would probably find a general lack of confidence in the reconstituted institutions of government combined with a heightened concern about sectarian status and security. This reality should be taken into consideration when discussing the propensity for interaction with Palestinians.

Table 8.5 Relationship between religious background and communication with Maronites, in percentages (N=642)

	G-C N=95	G-O N=91	Sunnis N=161	Shi'ites N=240	Druze N=65
High	62	60	34	38	29
Medium	32	36	35	42	51
Low	6	4	31	20	17

Tolerance for Palestinians

All the attitudes contained in this battery of questions are regarded as negative or hostile to the Palestinians as a group, and this hypothesis is generally borne out by the statistical results. Such attitudes were intended to represent varying degrees of discrimination, ranging from simple avoidance to suppression or attack, with intermediate actions of exclusion and segregation. In order to cover many forms of discrimination, a list of the major areas in which it occurs was used in the formulation of items. These areas are: residence, education, marriages and the country. Drawing on lessons from the conflict in Northern Ireland, Brenan[4] suggests that antagonisms are checked for through mechanisms of avoidance, selective contact and functional integration. The mechanism of avoidance can be seen as a form of segregation. The best example of this form is found in education, housing and intermarriage. The basic argument behind the adoption of this set of questions is that in order for Palestinian resettlement to be feasible, Lebanese groups should show a high level of tolerance toward the Palestinians as a group.

Once again, it was expected that the Sunnis would display the lowest level of anti-Palestinianism, due to the religious bond that links the two groups.

Table 8.6 Relationship between religious background and accepting Palestinian neighbors, in percentages (N=1,065)

	Maronites N=307	G-C N=110	G-O N=100	Sunnis N=189	Shi'ites N=286	Druze N=73
Yes	40	51	42	51	57	50
No	47	43	46	38	39	41
Unsure	13	6	12	11	4	9

Cramer's V = 0.13
Alpha = 0.05

Table 8.7 Relationship between religious background and living in a Palestinian neighborhood, in percentages (N=1,060)

	Maronites N=307	G-C N=107	G-O N=101	Sunnis N=191	Shi'ites N=281	Druze N=73
Yes	7	13	15	36	24	33
No	84	81	74	51	71	58
Unsure	9	6	11	13	6	10

Cramer's V = 0.21   Alpha = 0.05

The Socio-Economic Integration of Palestinians

Integrated housing, where different groups live side by side, is believed to lessen prejudice, compared to segregated housing or the regional separation of minority groups.[5] Segregated housing also results in segregation in much else. It means, for example, that children go to schools attended largely or entirely by members of their own group. In Lebanon, Rosemary Sayyigh finds that evidence from third-generation refugees in Lebanon indicates marked discrimination in universities, the work place and social life: the result is the presence of uncrossable boundaries.[6]

Julie Peteet offers an American comparison:

> Palestinian refugees have been pathologized in a manner reminiscent of turn-of-the-century American hyperbole that immigrants carried tuberculosis. Segregating Palestinians would facilitate normalization of post-war Lebanon with national health restored through the isolation of an infectious presence.[7]

The first question (table 8.6) regarding residential integration was: "Would you accept Palestinians living in your neighborhood?" This question is designed to tap respondents' perceptions of Palestinians and whether they consider residential contact a threat because "Palestinians residing in their neighborhood" may result in tension or hostility. The responses show that 50 percent of the respondents do not consider living side-by-side with Palestinians a menace, as opposed to 41 percent who do (see table 8.6). By contrast, as shown in table 8.7, only one-fifth of respondents would accept "living in a Palestinian neighborhood." Since violent clashes inside Palestinian camps are frequently reported, fears of endangering their own life and property perhaps explain Lebanese respondents' desire to avoid such Palestinian localities. In the past, refugee camps were scattered among the different Lebanese regions, and some, like Shatila and Bourj al-Barajneh in Beirut, and Ain al-Hilweh in Sidon, had merged with surrounding Lebanese areas. Contacts between the camp population and Lebanese were frequent and normal. People did not seek deliberately to avoid contact with Palestinians, as they do today.

Table 8.8 Relationship between religious background and Lebanese students attending same schools with Palestinians, in percentages (N=1,050)

	Maronites N=306	G-C N=106	G-O N=101	Sunnis N=190	Shi'ites N=283	Druze N=73
Same Schools	27	28	30	61	49	70
Separate Schools	61	55	50	30	40	19
Unsure	12	17	21	9	11	11

Cramer's V = 0.23   Alpha = 0.05

Table 8.9 Relationship between religious background and sending Lebanese students to Palestinian schools, in percentages (N=1,061)

	Maronites N=306	G-C N=110	G-O N=99	Sunnis N=191	Shi'ites N=282	Druze N=73
Yes	14	18	21	51	37	55
No	78	76	72	41	58	40
Unsure	8	6	7	8	5	6

Cramer's V = 0.21
Alpha = 0.05

The importance of friendship across group lines on inter-group relations is identified by Cook[8] who maintained that inter-group friendship reduces racial prejudice and discrimination and promotes "the generalization of positive affects felt toward other ethnic friends." Reich and Purbhoo[9] found that school contact improved cross-group role-taking ability among both minority and majority Canadians, suggesting that inter-group friendship may generate cross-group empathy.

The survey also asked: "Do you think that Lebanese and Palestinian students should go to the same schools?" Some 43 percent favored common schools and 45 percent preferred separate schools (table 8.8). To understand the findings, one must remember that Lebanese schools tend to promote the dominant culture of the society while undermining other cultures. In Palestinian schools, the Palestinian history of struggles and revolution tends to dominate and provides the means by which a revolutionary consciousness is inculcated.[10] This explains Christian and Muslim avoidance of common schools, as attested by table 8.9, since many among them do not identify with the Palestinian cause.

Table 8.10 Relationship between religious background and accepting a relative having intimate relations with Palestinians, in percentages (N=1,060)

	Maronites N=307	G-C N=109	G-O N=101	Sunnis N=190	Shi'ites N=281	Druze N=72
Yes	26	35	27	55	37	44
No	58	54	58	26	52	46
Unsure	15	11	15	18	10	10

Cramer's V = 0.18
Alpha = 0.05

The Socio-Economic Integration of Palestinians

Table 8.11 Relationship between religious background and accepting a relative marrying a Palestinian, in percentages (N=1,058)

	Maronites N=305	G-C N=108	G-O N=100	Sunnis N=101	Shi'ites N=282	Druze N=72
Yes	18	21	17	48	29	3
No	54	53	51	25	47	36
Unsure	28	26	32	27	24	31

Cramer's V = 0.19
Alpha = 0.05

Table 8.12 Relationship between religious background and government banning intermarriages, in percentages (N=1,059)

	Maronites N=305	G-C N=109	G-O N=100	Sunnis N=190	Shi'ites N=283	Druze N=72
Yes	32	28	34	6	16	13
No	56	57	53	82	70	83
Unsure	12	16	13	13	14	4

Cramer's V = 0.19
Alpha = 0.05

Next, respondents were presented with a question on their readiness to accept intimate relations with Palestinians. Only one-third were unfavorable to this prospect as attested by table 8.10.

Respondents were also asked: "Would you accept a relative of yours marrying a Palestinian?" One-third said yes; approximately half said no (see table 8.11). While the percentage saying yes may seem low, it fits into the context in which most people marry within the same religious faith, and, probably within the same sectarian group. It is also noteworthy that proposals for introducing civil marriage in 1998 came under scathing attack from spiritual leaders representing all Lebanese communities, except those of the Druze sect. Therefore, if Lebanese wish to marry outside their religious faith, it is impossible to do so without either converting or becoming a religious "dissident."

The Christians' response to the far more stringent question in table 8.12, that of banning intermarriage with a Palestinian, may seem to indicate religious prejudice. In this case, however, a difference of faith is only part of the story: the long legacy of bloodshed between Christians and Palestinians undoubtedly also contributes to this attitude.

The Socio-Economic Integration of Palestinians

The position on Palestinian civil rights

Table 8.13 Relationship between religious background and excluding Palestinians from Lebanon, in percentages (N=1,006)

	Maronite N=300	G-C N=104	G-O N=93	Sunnis N=178	Shi'ites N=261	Druze N=70
Yes	88	80	75	37	62	54
Somewhat no	11	14	25	47	33	41
No	1	6	—	16	6	6

Cramer's V = 0.30
Alpha = 0.05

Table 8.14 Relationship between religious background and granting Palestinians basic rights, in percentages (N=946)

	Maronites N=256	G-C N=91	G-O N=85	Sunnis N=177	Shi'ites N=267	Druze N=71
Citizenship	3	8	2	15	9	10
Civic and social rights	63	59	62	75	69	82
No rights	34	33	35	10	23	9

Cramer's V = 0.19
Alpha = 0.05

Naturally, an overwhelming majority of the respondents – namely Christian groups – would like to see Palestinian refugees deported out of the country (see table 8.13). But until a political solution is reached, the refugees have been pressuring the government to grant them civil rights. What are Lebanese respondent preferences in regard to this particular issue? The main instrument in any integration policy is a general welfare policy: healthcare, social benefits, free education in comprehensive schools and access to higher education and labor-market policies.[11] The labor market is a key arena when it comes to integration. This is where migrants and natives of the host country meet, interact and develop mutual interdependence. Thus, work is seen as a principal instrument for achieving social integration. Immigrants who are permanent residents are recognized as enjoying the same rights and obligations as native citizens.

In view of the refugees' treatment by Lebanese authorities – whose implicit goal is to make sure that Palestinians are not integrated in the society – we expected Lebanese respondents to be unanimously opposed to granting refugees basic and civic rights. Yet an overwhelming majority of the respondents (68%) agreed that Palestinians in Lebanon should be enti-

The Socio-Economic Integration of Palestinians

tled to social and economic rights(see table 8.14). And while they blamed the Arabs and the United Nations Relief and Works Agency (UNRWA) for their deteriorating conditions, Christian groups were more reluctant to acknowledge this Palestinian claim to civil rights. Muslims, on the other hand, felt that Lebanon must share part of the responsibility for the refugees' current condition.

In line with Lebanese respondents' preference, there have been calls by many intellectuals to improve the official treatment of the refugees. For instance, lawyer Fadi Moghaizel urged the government to update the laws pertaining to Palestinian refugees on Lebanese soil. He distinguished between granting Palestinians civil rights and citizenship:

> We're not talking about integration. Palestinians don't want that and neither do we. But this does not stand in the way of giving them their minimum rights. There is a middle ground, and unless they get these rights they won't be able to continue their struggle or return to their home. Instead they will turn to crime . . . Unless their basic rights are secured, Lebanon loses as well. Palestinians must be helped so that they can wait decently until they return home . . . The Palestinians who work in Lebanon are forced to contribute to social security but without receiving any of its benefits. This is because there is no reciprocal arrangements as there is no Palestinian state . . . Palestinians here live like foreigners, but they don't have an embassy protecting them.[12]

Similarly, others concur that labor or economic dilemmas could be partially alleviated by allowing Palestinian doctors or lawyers to at least work in their own camps – especially if one considers the labor dilemma caused by the recent influx of Syrian workers who compete for work traditionally undertaken by the Palestinians.[13]

According to these views, the international community shares the burden along with the Lebanese, especially in ensuring financial support. The deteriorating state of Palestinians results from various factors, but the mainly financial difficulties plaguing UNRWA, and the lack of funds from the Palestinian Liberation Organization:

> Funding cannot and should not come from Lebanon, because it does not have the means. We're in an economic crisis. But Lebanon can help by having the proper laws that would enable Palestinians to work and move within society without competing with Lebanese. This doesn't require cash; it requires more cooperation from Lebanon and smoother formalities between the social security fund and UNRWA, for example . . . The funding of UNRWA has decreased dramatically, so there are more health problems and Palestinians' education levels have dropped . . . [something that] used to be their main passport to finding work abroad.[14]

The preceding review has shown that barriers to the socio-economic integration of the sizable Palestinian community into Lebanese society exist among the host population, albeit to varying degrees. Christians are manifestly more reluctant to tolerate Palestinians than their Muslim counterparts. Unexpectedly, though, there is a shared consensus on granting the refugees their basic rights, in a clear opposition to the Lebanese government's actual strategy. Furthermore, granting Palestinians their civil rights is welcomed by a portion of Lebanese, namely the Muslims. Granting Palestinians their civic rights would serve to alleviate their socio-economic situation in Lebanon and reduce the country's economic problems.

These attitudes are expected to have an impact on the resettlement of Palestinians in the country in the event of its imposition on Lebanon. Chapter 9 details popular attitudes toward implantation or resettlement.

Notes

1. G. W. Allport, *The Nature of Prejudice* (Cambridge, MA: Addison Wesley, 1954), pp. 268–69.
2. See, for example, B. Ann Bettancourt and Nancy Dorr, "Cooperative Interaction and Intergroup Bias: Effects of numerical representation and cross-cut role assignment," *Personality and Social Psychology Bulletin* 24(12) (December 1998), p. 1276.
3. Salma Husseini, *Redistribution de la Population du Liban pendant la Guerre Civile (1975–1988)*, unpublished PhD thesis, EHESS (Ecole des Hautes Etudes en Sciences Sociales), Paris, June 1992.
4. Paul Brenan, *The Conflict in Northern Ireland* (Paris, Longman, 1995).
5. Allport, *The Nature of Prejudice.*
6. Rosemary Sayyigh, "Dis/Solving the Refugee Problem," *Middle East Report* (Summer 1998), pp. 22–3
7. Julie Peteet, "Palestinians in Post-War Lebanon: From refugees to minority," *Middle East Report* (July-September 1996), p. 28
8. S.W. Cook, "Cooperative Interaction in Multiethnic Contexts," in N. Miller and M. B. Brewer (eds.), *Groups in Contact: The psychology of desegregation* (Orlando, FL: Academic Press, 1984), pp. 175–83.
9. C. Reich and M. Purbhoo, 1975, "The Effects of Cross-Cultural Contact," *Canadian Journal of Behavioral Scienc* 7, pp. 313–27.
10. Khalil Nakhle, "Palestinian Intellectuals and Revolutionary Transformation," in Khalil Nakhle and Elia Zureik (eds.), *The Sociology of the Palestinians* (London: Croom Helm, 1980), p. 195.
11. Charles Westin, "The Effectiveness of Settlement and Integration Policies Toward Immigrants and Their Descendants in Sweden," *International Migration Papers* 34, Migration Branch, ILO, Geneva, 2001.
12. Nadine Alfa, "Allowing Refugees their Rights Won't Adversely Affect the Country", *The Daily Star*, April 24,1998.
13. Saade, Wissam "Rafdukum al Tawtin Laisa bi Rafd" (Rejecting Implantation is not a Rejection), *An-Nahar,* November 12, 1999.
14. Nadine Alpha, "Allowing Refugees their Rights."

9

The Origins and Nature of Popular Attitudes toward Resettlement

This chapter investigates Lebanese respondents' attitudes toward an imposed Palestinian settlement in the country. Specifically, the study focuses on: (1) views on naturalization; (2) implications of resettlement domestically; (3) proposed resumption of civil war; (4) expected course of action to oppose resettlement; and (5) position on an imposed settlement.

Views on Naturalization

Table 9.1 Relationship between religious background and views on Lebanon's naturalization decree, in percentages (N=1,043)

	Maronites N=306	G-C N=106	G-O N=97	Sunnis N=184	Shi'ites N=277	Druze N=73
Decree is appropriate	1	5	1	11	4	3
Decree is too rigid	30	43	50	52	40	47
Decree should be ceased	69	52	50	37	56	51

Cramer's V = 0.19
Alpha = 0.05

A review of the respondents' views of the Lebanese naturalization decree (table 9.1) is imperative due to its latent policy implications regarding scenarios for Palestinian resettlement in Lebanon. An estimated 400,000 people were granted citizenship as a result of the 1994 decree, which the Maronite League opposed on the basis that it granted citizenship to undeserving applicants. The decree was at the time opposed by Lebanese from all faiths. The Maronite patriarch, Cardinal Nasrallah Sfeir, also blocked attempts to enact a new, controversial, follow-up decree.

Responses to the question concerning the appropriateness of the naturalization code reveal the controversial nature of this issue in Lebanese politics. Only 4% of the respondents felt that the nationalization decree was appropriate. By contrast, 41% said it was too rigid and 55% that it should be repealed. Obviously, the sharp political divisions among Lebanese foes appear clearly in the respondents' views on naturalization.

One would expect the views on the naturalization decree to be influenced by the respondents' religious affiliation, and cross-tabulation of the two variables revealed interesting relationships between religion and views on the subject. Sunnis, Shi'ites and Druze were more vehemently opposed to naturalization than their Maronite, Catholic and Orthodox counterparts, with the former believing the decree was too rigid and needing revision. Conversely, respondents from all Lebanese groups were more inclined than the Sunnis to demand a full repeal of the decree.

Greek-Catholic and Greek-Orthodox respondents seem to side with the Maronites on this particular proposal. In Zahlé, an overwhelmingly Catholic region, the Melchite Bishop claimed that the government was encouraging 50,000 Christians from Syria, Jordan and other countries to apply for citizenship even though they had no intention of living in Lebanon and therefore would be of no benefit to the country or its economy. He said that their usefulness, if the plan was a serious proposition, would be as an effort to compensate for the uneven additions of Muslims through naturalization.[1]

Table 9.2 Relationship between religious background and major deficiency in naturalization decree, in percentages (N=998)

	Maronites N=306	G-C N=106	G-O N=97	Sunnis N=184	Shi'ites N=277	Druze N=73
Granted citizenship to Palestinians	24	22	22	9	14	9
Different reasons	76	78	78	91	86	91

Cramer's V = 0.16   Alpha = 0.05

One major deficiency in the naturalization decree was that a substantial majority of the population felt that that it did not guarantee Lebanon's national interests. Only a minority of the respondents felt that the problem was the alleged naturalization of a few thousand Palestinians.[2] By the same token (see table 9.2) a few respondents attributed the major deficiency in the naturalization decree to its exclusion of Lebanese emigrants' right to citizenship. For years, there have been arguments, mainly from Christian politicians, that Lebanese emigrants should be able to vote in elections through the embassies of their countries. At present, citizens residing

Popular Attitudes toward Resettlement

abroad must return to Lebanon to cast their votes. The aim was to preserve the estimated balance of the population. Compared to the results depicted by the 1994 study, respondents of all sects seem to maintain an increasingly negative attitude toward the naturalization decree. The pattern of the responses could be explained by several factors:

1. Analysts and politicians have increasingly focused on the negative aspects of the decree. For this purpose, several conferences were held to discuss the implications of the decree on Lebanon. While all participants in these meetings agreed on the adverse repercussions of naturalization, they also have used this question to discredit the previous government (the president Elias Hrawi mandate 1989–98), which was responsible for its enactment.
2. The media has extensively portrayed the Palestinian refugee presence "as a time bomb expected to detonate at any time, causing the disintegration of Lebanese society."
3. Actual official Lebanese statements serve to mobilize the public against attempts at naturalization.
4. President Elias Hrawi's intention, toward the end of his mandate (1989–98), to enact a supplement to the 1994 decree and the wide opposition and antagonism it created.
5. Interior Minister Michel Murr stated that a new clause had been added to the naturalization draft law to prevent Palestinians from gaining citizenship. This change was intended to quell the fears of some groups such as the Maronite League, Murr said. Also, Israeli Premier Ehud Barak's statement raised fears in Lebanon that the Lebanese would have to pay the price for a regional settlement.[3]

Table 9.3 Relationship between religious background and implication of resettlement on domestic situation, in percentages (N=1,049)

	Maronites N=307	G-C N=106	G-O N=97	Sunnis N=182	Shi'ites N=284	Druze N=73
Will cause damaging repercussions	69	59	55	26	48	37
Will cause no worthwhile repercussions	25	33	27	40	36	40
Unsure of the impact of resettlement	6	9	19	35	16	23

Cramer's V = 0.24   Alpha = 0.05

Popular Attitudes toward Resettlement

The Lebanese public's opposition to resettlement has been guided by the recognition that such a move would alter the precarious foundations of Lebanese society. More specifically, the arguments for the current attitude rest on three major assumptions: First, arguments against resettlement are based on the belief that it will affect the delicate political make-up of the Lebanese system. This assumption follows from the recognition that mass naturalization of Palestinians will tip the country's sectarian balance, which will have tremendous political repercussions.

Table 9.4 Relationship between religious affiliation and projection of the nature of damaging repercussions of Palestinian resettlement, in percentages (N=1,038)

	Maronites N=305	G-C N=105	G-O N=99	Sunnis N=184	Shi'ites N=274	Druze N=71
Will upset Lebanon's demographic ecology	31	33	34	33	32	23
Will aggravate Lebanon's economic crisis	10	13	12	21	19	39
Threatens power-sharing	56	50	49	25	41	27
No result	3	4	5	22	8	11

Cramer's V = 0.20
Alpha = 0.05

Second, the argument against resettlement has to do with the resumption of the civil war. The stationing of Palestinian guerrillas on Lebanese soil had already prompted one devastating and costly war. Permanent settlement of the refugees threatens to recall memories of the past.

Finally, the arguments against resettlement rest on the assumption that such a development will have negative economic repercussions. This point receives additional importance as Lebanon's post-war economy suffers enormously (it currently faces an estimated $30 billion foreign debt). Consequently, Lebanese groups are predicted to negatively perceive the consequences of the permanent settlement of Palestinian refugees.

Table 9.3 provides information on what respondents perceive as the repercussions of resettlement. Note that almost nine out of every ten respondents foresee damaging repercussions. This question was probed

Popular Attitudes toward Resettlement

further in an effort to acquire more detailed information regarding the respondents' opposition to resettlement. Thus, in response to an open-ended contingency question on what actually motivated them to oppose resettlement, many respondents made a number of projections. These are given in table 9.4.

On average, 43% of the respondents said resettlement will have a disruptive effect on Lebanon's socio-political balance. Lebanese scholar Joseph Maila concedes that the permanent settlement of the Palestinian refugees in Lebanon – the vast majority of whom are Sunni – could be fatal to the country's social mosaic.[4] The Palestinians, he says, could become an independent sectarian group, a development unprecedented in Lebanon. The linkage between these Palestinians and the Palestinian Authority is thus also likely to create problems for the Lebanese in the coming years.

The second worry was economic: It was mentioned by 49% of respondents. Opponents of Palestinian resettlement have always justified their position on economic grounds, pointing to Lebanon's chronic social and economic crisis. According to the data provided by the UN survey, 41% of Lebanese adults have expressed a willingness to emigrate. In fact, 22% said they had already applied for emigration. One major cause cited for this desire to leave the country was unemployment, which reached 27% in 2000.[5]

Proposed resumption of the civil war as a result of resettlement

Table 9.5 Relationship between religious background and proposed resumption of civil war, in percentages (N=1,057)

	Maronites N=306	G-C N=109	G-O N=97	Sunnis N=189	Shi'ites N=282	Druze N=73
Yes	66	62	57	22	44	22
No	16	18	22	60	37	63
Unsure	18	20	22	18	19	15

Cramer's V = 0.28
Alpha = 0.05

The permanent presence of Palestinians in Lebanon worries a substantial portion of the Lebanese population, especially Christians. Moreover, the government's involuntary acquiescence in the presence of armed Palestinians in the refugee camps exacerbates this view.[6] The pro-Arafat and Palestinian rejectionists refuse to hand over their weapons in the absence of a clear understanding with Lebanese authorities concerning the camps: "Weapons may be needed to cope with particular instances," says Shafiq Hout,[7] the PLO's former representative in Beirut. Fear and a sense of equal treatment lead Christians likewise to hold on to arms. The net result: A high degree of expectation exists that a permanent Palestinian presence would mean a new civil war, as expressed by 47 percent of the respondents (see table 9.5).

The possibility that Palestinian guerillas would launch uncontrolled and uncontrollable attacks after Israel unilaterally withdrew from south Lebanon in May 2000, triggered mixed reactions from Lebanese politicians. For Dory Chamoun,[8] president of the National Liberal Party, President Emile Lahoud's statement that the government has no role in guaranteeing the security of the camps "disregards citizens' feelings opposing Palestinian operations." Interpreted as an implicit invitation from Syria for Palestinian groups to assert themselves, the waging of military operations by non-Lebanese would endanger Lebanon's position and risk international isolation.

For the Lebanese, there is a crucial difference between Lebanese resistance to liberate an occupied territory and Palestinian operations at a time when Israeli–Palestinian talks were under way. The Lebanese vividly remember Palestinian cross-border operations in the 1970s, moves that prompted severe Israeli retaliation and contributed to the outbreak of the civil war. While other Arab–Israeli borders are stable, and while diplomatic negotiations are under way between Israel and many Arab countries, the Lebanese feel strongly that Palestinian operations against Israel should not be launched from Lebanon.

Expected course of action against an imposed settlement

Table 9.6 Relationship between religious background and expected course of action, in percentages (N=1,008)

	Maronites N=299	G-C N=103	G-O N=96	Sunnis N=169	Shi'ites N=269	Druze N=72
Acquiesce	23	28	27	44	26	26
Protest nonviolently	52	44	51	49	59	61
Resist militarily	26	28	22	7	16	1

Cramer's V = 0.16
Alpha = 0.05

Political attitudes and perceptions are expected to have important behavioral consequences. This is not only applicable to democracies but is common to all political systems. What course of action are Lebanese citizens willing to take in the event of Palestinian resettlement being imposed on Lebanon – especially if they perceive this action as a threat to national interests and security? Would they comply with it or confront its imposition? A battery of questions was devised in order to tap respondents' type and extent of protest or their compliance with this (see tables 9.6, 9.7 and 9.8). We assumed that Lebanese respondents tend to oppose the permanent settlement of refugees using peaceful means and that only a minority would resort to illegal and violent means.

Notwithstanding a true mobilization and a commitment to strong political parties and leaders, only a minority of Lebanese expressed willingness to take part in military activities to prevent the imposition of Palestinian settlement in Lebanon. However, this does not mean the Lebanese would passively accept Palestinian permanent settlement, a fact confirmed by a September 1999 conference of Lebanese spiritual leaders, aimed at foiling any permanent settlement. In addition, a range of Lebanese political forces joined Chamoun's call for a national convention to take joint action or necessary nonviolent steps to resist settlement.[9]

Table 9.7 Relationship between religious background and likelihood of action, in percentages (N=998)

	Maronites N=300	G-C N=107	G-O N=96	Sunnis N=162	Shi'ites N=264	Druze N=69
Yes	65	60	64	43	64	61
No	9	18	15	25	7	15
Unsure	26	22	22	33	29	25

Cramer's V = 0.15
Alpha = 0.05

Table 9.8 Relationship between religious background and expected success of action, in percentages (N=1,006)

	Maronites N=302	G-C N=103	G-O N=95	Sunnis N=169	Shi'ites N=268	Druze N=69
Yes	47	48	48	31	52	41
No	26	18	17	30	24	13
Unsure	27	34	40	35	25	46

Cramer's V = 0.16   Alpha = 0.05

All six communal groups show a low predisposition toward armed action, something that has to do in part with the increased jurisdiction assumed by Lebanese authorities (see tables 9.6, 9.7, and 9.8). The Ta'if Accord established a modicum of security in much of the country, and Lebanese citizens have since grown increasingly accustomed to the authority of the Lebanese state. They are thus less likely to resort to violence to resolve conflicts.

Expected political impact of resettlement

Within this agreement, however, there are differences. Most Lebanese Christians see the Palestinian presence as an infringement on the country's sovereignty; thus, during the civil war, right-wing Christian parties were the first to clash with Palestinian guerilias. In contrast, Lebanese Muslims, especially Shi'ites, clearly disapprove of violence against Palestinians, perhaps because they, like the Palestinians, are engaged in a conflict with Israel.

Table 9.9 Relationship between religious background and attitude toward Ta'if Accord, in percentages (N=1,046)

	Maronites N=299	G-C N=108	G-O N=97	Sunnis N=186	Shi'ites N=283	Druze N=73
Yes	22	19	28	53	38	48
No	62	58	49	29	43	32
Unsure	16	22	24	18	19	21

Cramer's V = 0.2   Alpha = 0.05

The presence of democratic political systems is often stressed as the basic means to avoid the outbreak of ethnic strife and warfare in ethnically heterogeneous or generally unstable political units. For example, in an undemocratic and intrinsically oppressive system such as the former Yugoslavia, striving for greater national autonomy split the country into hostile minority groups. In other countries, such as Armenia and Azerbaijan, long-standing national enmities re-emerged in the absence of a shared national identity. Is Palestinian resettlement likely to reignite the age-old political conflict among the Lebanese?

Table 9.10 Relationship between religious background and alternative political solution, in percentages (N=659)

	Maronites N=222	G-C N=80	G-O N=69	Sunnis N=85	Shi'ites N=169	Druze N=34
Decentralization	61	68	59	20	25	56
Religious state	5	3	4	9	5	—
Authoritarian state	2	3	1	11	5	3
Other	32	28	35	60	64	41

Cramer's V = 0.23   Alpha = 0.05

Popular Attitudes toward Resettlement

To this end, respondents were asked: "As a consequence of Palestinian settlement (in case Palestinian settlement should be imposed) would you continue to support the Ta'if Accord?" Only 34 percent said yes; 47 percent said no (see table 9.9) . The 1989 agreement, also known as the Document of National Understanding, ended fifteen years of civil war in Lebanon and established internal conditions for peace. Ta'if not only attempted to achieve intercommunal equilibrium, but embraced a consensual, sectarian logic, dictating procedures that distributed public offices among the various communities, providing communities with a veto, and regulating conflicting sectarian interests.

Basically, although not all parties consented to the accord, its imposition as a solution in the form of communal contract was made possible because no party or community emerged victorious during the war, and also because – in the absence of facts from a nationwide census – no community could claim proof of a demographic majority. Maintaining the peace, therefore, was and is a matter of maintaining a balance of sharing power and of preserving the rights of communities that view themselves as the bedrock on which the Lebanese state is constructed.[10]

Under the existing political arrangement, however, most Christians feel politically underrepresented, alienated and excluded both from the government and from the Christian parties that have accepted the new order while continuing to dissent on details. In the past, the "Palestinization" of the country prompted Lebanese Christians to take up arms and think the unthinkable: an alliance with Israel and a full commitment to partition. Palestinian settlement would push the Christians to bring forward fair, just and equal representation in the system in the light of new demographic shifts.[11] It is also assumed that Palestinian settlement would tip the sectarian balance in the country, leading to an increased Sunni population. This would lead to demands for increased political representation for the Sunni community which would, in a sense, become dominant. In turn, this could aggravate the situation for other groups.

Sunni respondents, more than any others, seem to accept the legitimacy of the Ta'if arrangement. Under it, the Sunni community recovered some "weight" in Lebanon, with the resurgence of the older upper class, the eclipse of the militias, Maronite misfortunes and an enhanced role for a Sunni prime minister.

Although the Shi'ites won on the political level, achieving greater visibility and enlarged participation compared to their marginalized position in the pre-war period, there are important numbers of Shi'ites who feel that the Sunni community has been the major beneficiary of the Ta'if reforms. These Shi'ites fear that any settlement of the (mainly Sunni) Palestinians will further strengthen Sunni political power.

Druze support for the actual political arrangement depends on continuous benefits in terms of political power and resources. Currently, the Druze community maintains a political position beyond its demographic strength. If that position is subject to change, their preferred option is decentralization, which they experienced in the Chouf mountains between 1983 and 1990 (see table 9.10). Given their small numbers, their second option is a secular, de-confessionalized state where they would be able to gain an important share in politics.

An imposed settlement

What about the future? As noted earlier, the question of Palestinian resettlement has been the subject of increasing discussion by Lebanese political figures and by the Lebanese media. Four questions pertaining to this debate were used in this study. The aim was to account for the respondents' familiarity with this critical issue, which receives greater public attention than the Lebanese government's controversial plans for reconstruction, political reform or economic privatization.

The results of the responses to these questions are presented in tables 9.11, 9.12, 9.13 and 9.14. Certainly, a number of respondents do not know whether Palestinians will be repatriated or settled (table 9.11 and 9.12); they are nevertheless quick to point out their opposition to the latter (table 9.13). Opposition to settlement also appears to cut across the religious affiliations of the respondents, and this is the declared position of all political forces and religious authorities in the country. There are slight variations between Sunni and Christian respondents, particularly the Maronites: The former leads in support and the latter in opposition. Should some of those giving "unsure" responses among the Sunnis turn out to support settlement, the Palestinian issue could well become divisive in Lebanon's sectarian politics.

Table 9.11 Relationship between religious background and plans for resettlement, in percentages (N=1,062)

	Maronites N=308	G-C N=109	G-O N=99	Sunnis N=189	Shi'ites N=284	Druze N=73
Yes	72	76	82	72	68	78
No	20	19	12	22	25	19
Unsure	8	5	6	6	7	3

Tables 9.11 and 9.12 also shows that the regular Lebanese media reports of alleged US, Canadian or Israeli support for a Palestinian settlement scheme as part of the Arab–Israeli negotiations has made an impact. Lebanese respondents appear aware of these supposed efforts and widely reject such plans.

Popular Attitudes toward Resettlement

Table 9.12 Relationship between religious background and imposed resettlement (N=1,048)

	Maronites N=307	G-C N=107	G-O N=101	Sunnis N=191	Shi'ites N=281	Druze N=73
Yes	66	59	66	57	59	75
No	17	23	16	23	28	13
Unsure	18	18	18	21	14	13

Table 9.13 Relationship between religious background and accepting imposed resettlement, in percentages (N=1,052)

	Maronites N=303	G-C N=108	G-O N=99	Sunnis N=188	Shi'ites N=281	Druze N=72
Yes	4	7	8	27	11	15
No	84	79	73	48	74	72
Unsure	12	14	19	26	15	17

Cramer's V = 0.22
Alpha = 0.05

Table 9.14 Relationship between religious background and opinion likely to change in the future, in percentages (N=1,049)

	Maronites N=307	G-C N=107	G-O N=101	Sunnis N=191	Shi'ites N=281	Druze N=73
Yes	27	30	22	32	26	39
No	60	55	57	45	60	52
Unsure	14	15	20	23	13	9

Cramer's V = 0.11
Alpha = 0.05

The claim that foreign plots exist to impose the settlement of Palestinians on Lebanon has increased worries among Lebanese about the probability that Palestinian refugees may stay in the country indefinitely.[12] There is a widespread impression that the future of the Palestinians will be decided by the United States as the Arab–Israeli peace talks reach a decisive stage.

In fact, US proposals to settle refugees in Arab states have so far proven unworkable. They were met with official rejection in the case of Jordan's King Abdullah:[13] "Everybody wants to solve this problem but it will not be at the expense of Jordan." Thus the Gulf states also rejected the proposals as a potential danger to political stability.[14]

As permanent-status negotiations have resumed, the Palestinian

Authority (PA) has shown no enthusiasm for taking the Palestinians in Lebanon into a future Palestinian state. Interestingly, like Lebanon, Syria and Jordan, the PA considers itself one of the countries hosting refugees.[15] Palestinian President Yasser Arafat prefers to hold on to the Palestinians' right of return in order to keep the pressure on Israel and also because of economic obstacles facing those who want to relocate to the West Bank and Gaza Strip.

The official policy of the Lebanese government attempts to stimulate Palestinian emigration from Lebanon in order to leave the smallest possible remaining Palestinian demographic and political burden. Christian groups have been more reluctant to acknowledge Palestinian rights. The sectarian structure of the Lebanese political system, in which Christian Maronites were previously dominant, has prevented the acceptance of Palestinians into Lebanese society. This has continued to be the case even after the end of the civil war greatly reduced Maronite political dominance.

While the Maronites are concerned about the potential damage that Palestinian presence in Lebanon can do to their community, the Shi'ites in southern Lebanon have paid the price with fierce Shi'ite respondents' disaffection from the Palestinians clearly expressed. In fact, the majority of Shi'ites would like to see the Palestinians repatriated or resettled outside Lebanon. Hizbullah secretary-general Hassan Nasrallah's statement reinforces this: "The Palestinians should go back to Palestine, or if some international body proposes . . . take them out of Lebanon and distribute them among Syria, Iraq, Canada, Australia or other parts of the world."[16]

Those who insist on denying Palestinians their most essential rights justify their attitude on the basis of refusing resettlement. Accordingly, allowing Palestinians to improve their social and economic situation would enable Palestinians to assume the position of a community in the diaspora, like any other Arab community in Lebanon. The Lebanese government would be able to correct the anomalous situation of the Palestinians with its corresponding restrictions without considering such a step a move toward indirect resettlement.[17]

The Sunnis and the Druze seem the least affected by Palestinian resettlement. Among the respondents, Sunnis and Druze agreed more than any other group that Palestinians in Lebanon should be entitled to most social and economic rights. Conversely, only a slight minority felt that Palestinians should be eligible for citizenship, even though, a permanent Palestinian presence would give a tremendous boost to the political status of Lebanese Sunnis.

The Lebanese media has been emphasizing the government's worries concerning the future of the 360,000 Palestinian refugees in the country. The probability that they may be allowed to stay indefinitely has increased Lebanese suspicions.[18]

Popular Attitudes toward Resettlement

Druze leader Walid Jumblatt suggested in 1994 that several thousand Palestinians be thrown out of East Beirut and resettled in Qurai, a deserted village on the southern margin of the Chouf. Jumblatt received backing from Premier Rafik Hariri, who shared his opinion about the impracticality of expelling Palestinians from the country.[19] This expressed a common Druze–Sunni interest, a reality that seems to be confirmed by the present findings, since Sunni and Druze respondents appear more hospitable and open to the idea of resettlement than any other groups.

The other dimension of the problem is related to the disruptive impact of resettlement. Those who stress the political and historical reason for insisting on the deporation of the refugees emphasize the link between the presence of the Palestinians in Lebanon and the wars and troubles it has been through. They see in an armed Palestinian presence a dangerous impetus for another civil war. Today, Palestinian camps remain political and military "ghettos," each with several hundred armed men belonging to different Palestinian factions.

One proposed solution to the refugee problem is emigration to Western countries. In a study involving Palestinian refugees from the Ain al-Hilweh camp, Hilal Khashan[20] found that 98 percent of the respondents wished to emigrate to the West. That would also probably be the most popular alternative among the population at large. To date, Canada has offered to absorb 15,000 Palestinians.

Nonetheless, there will continue to be a significant Palestinian presence in Lebanon, and some very tentative steps have been taken to address this fact. In October 1992, Lebanese Foreign Minister Fares Boueiz stated that the permanent settlement of 50,000–100,000 Palestinians in Lebanon should be viewed as acceptable.[21] One suggestion was for a portion of the Palestinian community to have its legal status normalized through extended Palestinian citizenship, coupled with permanent residency status.[22] The US "green card" or the French "carte de sejour" could serve as a model: full civil and economic rights but not political rights (voting, office-holding), thus promoting socio-economic integration without hampering political stability.

Palestinians and Israelis approach the question of refugees and the right of return from radically different perspectives. The Palestinian narrative maintains that the Zionists forcibly expelled the Arab refugees in 1948. Palestinians thus insist on the right of the refugees to return to their homes, demanding that Israel unilaterally accept complete moral responsibility for the injustice of the refugees' expulsion. In contrast, the Israeli narrative rejects the refugee's right of return. Israel argues that it was the Arabs who caused the Palestinian refugee problem, by rejecting the creation of the state of Israel and declaring a war upon it – a war which, like most wars, created refugee problems, including a Jewish one. Yet Israel sees the return

Popular Attitudes toward Resettlement

of the Palestinian refugees as an existential threat insofar as it would undermine the Jewish character and the viability of the state. In the middle ground, Arab host countries, including Lebanon, deny any responsibility on this issue.

This chapter aimed at understanding how Lebanese citizens view the Palestinians resident in their country, and especially the prospect that they might settle permanently there. Most Lebanese are aware of the ongoing debate over Palestinian settlement in the country; they tend to oppose the idea, and call for preventing its imposition. All Lebanese groups showed a lack of enthusiasm to "resettling the Palestinians" in the sense of granting them citizenship and political rights. Most Lebanese communities view the Palestinians as a major destabilizing force capable of upsetting the precarious sectarian imbalance of inter-group relations, and possibly even bringing about a renewal of civil war. Hence, for most Lebanese the question is about their own political survival, not Palestinian resettlement. If the actual perceptions stand, resettlement would create the potential for communal conflict and would affect the social cohesion of the society.

Notes

1. *The Daily Star*, November 7, 1998.
2. According to Colonel Chawki Khalifa, a former officer in the Lebanese Surete Generale, who participated in preparing for the decree, only 5,795 Palestiians were eligible for citizenship which was granted to around 30,0000. See *Lubnan bainal geopolitik al-Israiili wa al-dimografia al filastiniah* (Lebanon Between Israel's Geopolitics and Palestinian Demographics), (Beirut, 2002).
3. *An-Nahar*, July 28, 1999
4. *An-Nahar*, February 25, 2000.
5. Naamatullah Abi-Nasr, former President of the Maronite League, "Lebanese Identity: Between naturalization and implantation," conference at the University of Saint Esprit (Kaslik, Lebanon), November 26, 1999.
6. Hilal Khashan and Simon Haddad, "The Coupling of the Syrian–Lebanese Peace Tracks: Beirut's options," *Security Dialogue* 30(2) (June 2000), pp. 201–14.
7. Murr Television (Beirut), November 8, 1999.
8. *An-Nahar*, April 13, 2000
9. *Mideast Mirror*, September 1, 1999.
10. See Joseph Maila, "The Ta'if Accord: An evaluation," *Peace For Lebanon?*, pp. 31–44.
11. Naamatullah Abi-Nasr, former president of the Maronite League, "Lebanese Identity: Between naturalization and implantation," conference at the University of Saint Esprit (Kaslik, Lebanon), November 26, 1999.
12. *An-Nahar*, Beirut, July 29, 1999
13. *The Scotsman*, Edinburgh, October 7, 1999.
14. *Middle East Intelligence Bulletin*, January 2000.

15 Asad Abd ar-Rahman, chairman of the PLO Refugee Department, news conference, Ramallah, February 28, 1999.
16 *Middle East Insight*, February 2000, p. 1
17 Interview with Mahmoud Soueid, director of the Institute for Palestinian Studies in Beirut, November 25, 1999, MTV Television. Soueid stressed that granting Palestinians civil rights doesn't mean giving up their right to return because in Israel, Palestinians were given this right and they did not lose their identity. This proposition was during the "Conference on the Palestinians in Advanced Lebanon" at Oxford (1996). Those who supported granting "civil rights to Palestinians" maintained that if Palestinians were allowed to work in the formal sector they would contribute taxes to the state and thereby benefit the Lebanese economy.
18 On November 9, 1999, *An-Nahar* newspaper spoke of US plans to pressure Lebanon to accept a portion of its Palestinian community as permanent citizens. Later, the *International Herald Tribune,* December 13, 1999, again highlighted Lebanon's concerns toward its Lebanese population. In addition, numerous articles reported US and Canadian plans and involvement in preparing for resettlement have been reported in Lebanese media particularly in Al-Diyar, March 8 , 2000.
19 Sarkis Naum. "Settlement of Palestinians in Lebanon: National, sectarian and confessional consideration," *Al-Wasat*, August 29, 1994.
20 Hilal Khashan, "The Despairing Palestinians," *Journal of South Asian and Middle Eastern Studies* 16(1) (Fall 1992), p. 16.
21 *L'orient Le Jour* (Beirut), October 2, 1992.
22 Nawaf Salam, "Between Repatriation and Resettlement: Palestinian refugees in Lebanon," *The Journal of Palestine Studies* 2(1) (Autumn 1994), pp. 18–28.

10

Lebanese Perceptions of Palestinians

Previous research has revealed that positive, strong relationships across groups increase inter-group cooperation and mitigate inter-group conflict. In order for the Lebanese to have harmonious relations with Palestinians they should be able to manifest positive perceptions toward them. Obviously, as Lebanese views of Palestinians are negative, it is necessary to isolate the variables which have predictive impact and that play a role in extenuating the adverse perceptions. This chapter details as many of these variables as possible, so that they might contribute in furthering our understanding of Lebanese attitudes toward Palestinians and their status in the country.

Correlates of Attitudes toward Resettlement

The overall perceptions of Palestinians of the surveyed respondents are not impressive. Negative attitudes hinder and even sometimes disclose normal socio-political exchange with the Palestinian community. In an effort to trace those variables that may have some impact on Lebanese perceptions of Palestinians, bivariate probing for the following variables took place:

1. Communication with Palestinians.
2. Tolerance of Palestinians.[1]
3. Empathy with Palestinians.
4. Blaming Palestinians for war.

Because the predictor variables displayed significant intercorrelations with each other within each religious group, a test for multicolliniarity was conducted. Table 10.1 presents this matrix of bivariate correlations for the total sample. The correlations were all below 0.80, indicating that multicolliniarity was likely not a serious problem.

Lebanese Perceptions of Palestinians

Table 10.1 Relationship between perceptions of Palestinians and independent variables, by religious background

	Maronites N=308	G-C N=110	G-O N=101	Sunnis N=192	Shi'ites N=226	Druze N=73
Empathy	0.30	—	0.23	0.35	0.40	0.50
Blame for war	—	−0.41	—	−0.39	−0.46	−0.59
Communication	0.47	0.43	0.47	0.54	0.64	0.62
Tolerance	0.38	0.34	0.38	0.49	0.46	0.54

Table 10.2 Inter-item correlations between the independent variables

	Empathy	Blame for War	Communication	Tolerance
Empathy	1.00	0.48	0.55	0.55
Blame for war	0.48	1.00	0.46	0.47
Communication	0.55	0.46	1.00	0.65
Tolerance	0.54	0.47	0.65	1.00

Note: Correlation is significant at the 0.01 level.

Significant correlations (see table 10.1) were generated for the six confessional groups represented in the study. Immediately perceivable is the very stable relationship between perceptions of Palestinians on the one hand, and blame for war, communication, empathy and tolerance for Palestinians on the other. In any case, available social-psychological works on inter-group relations is forthright in predicting the moderating effect of inter-group empathy, contact and communication on intergroup acceptance and perceptions. In spite of this, the correlations render the evaluation of the coefficients of Lebanese groups' perceptions of Palestinians very complex, and an almost unyielding task. Apparently, inter-group perceptive criteria are incongruent as they vary from one group to another. However, bivariate correlations cannot indicate: (1) the total variation in communal perceptions of Palestinians among respondents explained by the independent variables, nor (2) the relative importance of the variables upon communal perceptions of Palestinians once the influence of competing variables has been controlled for.

Therefore, in order to manage the coefficients in a way that would measure the relative importance of the variables behind them, the stepwise regression procedure was applied to the data. This procedural choice rested on one important consideration: Theoretically, it was not possible to envision any particular independent variable which had conspicuously predictive qualities. The substantially significant correlations between communal perceptions of Palestinians and a number of independent variables attributed to the author's failure to rank-order these variables in a conceptual framework. The inability to delineate higher-order predictive variables precluded the application of the hierarchical inclusion procedure, and justified the use of stepwise regression.

Table 10.3 Multiple regression of factors influencing Lebanese perceptions of Palestinians

	Model 1	Model 2	Model 3	Model 4	Model 5
Age	—	—	—	—	—
Gender	—	—	—	−0.10 (3%)	—
SES	—	—	—	—	—
Religious Affiliation					
Maronites	—	—	—	—	—
Catholic	—	—	—	—	—
Orthodox	—	—	—	—	—
Sunnis	−0.40^2 (2%)	−0.10^2	—	—	—
Shi'ites	−0.15 (7%)	—	—	—	—
Druze	−0.26^2 (5%)	−0.08^1	—	—	—
Empathy	—	0.11^2 (1%)	0.10^2	—	—
Blame for war	—	−0.13 (3%)	−0.14 (3%)	−0.21^1 (4%)	−0.18^1 (2%)
Communication	0.40^2 (40%)	0.45^2 (38%)	0.45^2 (37%)	0.49^2 (41%)	
Tolerance	—	—	—	—	—
Perceptions of Sunnis	—	—	0.22 (5%)	—	0.24^2 (6%)
Perceptions of Maronites	—	—	—	−0.18^1 (1%)	−0.13^1 (2%)
R^2	0.14	0.44	0.46	0.45	0.51

Note: Table 10.3 shows standardized coefficients (betas) and percentages of variance (R^2) of the dependent variable explained or accounted for (perceptions of Palestinians) by the explanatory variables. $^1 p<0.05$. $^2 p<0.01$. Religious affiliation was included in the form of five "dummy" variables with Maronites being the reference category.

Bivariate correlations indicated that a number of independent variables (1–4, p. 118) were associated with perceptions of conflict with Palestinians (table 10.1), whether directly or inversely. Thus, in order to answer the research question concerning the independent relationship between the respondents' perceptions of Palestinians on the one hand, and social and political variables on the other, multiple regression analysis was employed. The analysis of the findings can be pursued along a two-facet paradigm that emerges from the multivariate application.

The first facet is connected with how much variance the regression equation explains. The higher the percentage of explained variance available, the more confident we can be in determining which independent variables cause which impact. Explanation of variance reduces uncertainty and improves predictability, which is the main objective of social research. Low variance levels signal extreme complexity and tend to belie that the study succeeded in uncovering the real causes of "Lebanese perceptions of Palestinians," or what needs to be done to improve them.

The second facet relates to the type and number of predictive variables. Table 10.3 presents coefficients of independent measures and socio-demographic controls (age, gender, socio-economic status, or SES, and religious denomination) on the dependent variable. As an initial step in the multivariate analysis, religion's influence is assessed by coding five of the six religious groups as dummy variables. Maronites who express the highest level of hostility toward Palestinians – more than any other religious group – serve as the reference category. The first model (Model 1) included only the control variables (i.e., demographics) and the religion dummy variables. The second model included the dummy variables, the control variables and the social interaction scale. Using these specifications, if socio-political factors are not taken into account, no significant effect is found for age, gender and SES. Significant effect, however, is found for all three Muslim denominations, which display a negative correlation with perceptions of Palestinians (Model 1).

However, once other independent variables are added to the equation (Model 2) none of the control variables bears significance, but the effect of sectarian denomination continues to be significant without contributing to the explanation of the variance. Communication with Palestinians accounted for 40% of the total variance; blame for war and empathy with Palestinians explained, respectively, only 3% and 1% of the total variance. Tolerance was found to be negligible in explaining Lebanese perceptions of Palestinians.

When communication with Sunnis was included in the regression equation of group relations with Palestinians, it explained only 5% of the total variance, while responsibility for war and communication conserved their strength (Model 3). Likewise, when communication with Maronites was included in the equation, it accounted for just 1% of the total variance, with communication and blame for war remaining significant (Model 4). In order to examine the impact of group relations with Maronites and Sunnis at the same time, communication with Maronites and Sunnis was incorporated in the equation (Model 5). Both variables accounted for 8% of the variance, while communication with Palestinians and blame retained significance. The rationale behind their inclusion was to expound the role of religious affinity in determining the intensity of Lebanese inter-group closeness.

However, the findings show that one explanatory variable emerges as particularly interesting for determining Lebanese respondents' perceptions: communication with Palestinians. Thus, the higher the respondents' frequency of communication, the more they feel closer to Palestinians. Indeed, these relationships are always stronger than those involving any other independent variable – i.e., empathy and responsibility for war were found weakly related to the criterion variable.

Some observations pertaining to other independent variables may be offered. Findings about these variables are not always consistent but are, in any event, of secondary importance to the present study. The first relates to the absence of the effect of tolerance on the respondents' perceptions; the second indicates that "empathy" appears to have a negligible effect on the respondents' perceptions.

The findings of the present study indicated that tolerance for Palestinians was an insignificant predictor variable for group relations with Palestinians. According to this concept, not only does an observer interpret a group or member of a group erroneously, but he or she concludes that the said member is inferior and therefore unwanted. This tendency for out-group rejection and hostility is clearly not reflected in the study's findings that a low rating of tolerance is related to hostility for Palestinians. Conversely, variables pertaining to Lebanon's internal group mechanisms and the nature of the socio-political conflict were more important in determining communal closeness to Palestinians.

One of the major consequences of the civil war was the confessional "cleansing" of Palestinian refugee camps in Christian-controlled areas to Muslim-controlled regions. Massive population shifts, accompanied by the reintegration of displaced Palestinians into more homogeneous, self-contained and exclusive spaces – and the consequent physical separations – have confined Palestinian interaction to practically two Lebanese groups, Sunni and Shi'ite Muslims.[2] However, a highly significant positive relationship between communication with Palestinians and views of Palestinians emerges from the findings.

In his attempt to determine the correlates of multiculturalism in

Australia, Robert Ho (1990) found that ethnocentrism was the only significant predictor, not any of the demographic variables, for respondents' attitudes toward multiculturalism. In the present survey, respondents' education, income and SES levels were, in most cases, unimportant predictors of communal closeness to Palestinians. Nevertheless, there are several interesting relationships, some of which identify promising areas for future research.

To begin with, the absence of any significant relationship involving SES deserves mention. It delineates the failure of the analysis to control for other meaningful factors, most notably the respondents' level of economic security and the perceived effect of Palestinian presence on employment opportunities and competition over economic issues. It delineates the failure of the analysis to control for other meaningful factors, most notably the perceived impact of the war on the respondents.

Coupled with the present study's findings that communication accounts for variance in Lebanese attitudes toward Palestinian resettlement, this suggests that a multi-factor model, including other variables pertaining to the Lebanese situation, has a much larger effect on views of Palestinians than do the respondents' self-interest measures. The tolerance scale itself would have been more revealing of the large and negative social distances corroborated between Lebanese groups on one hand, and the Palestinians on the other, if certain items representing extreme negative positions were included in the scale. For instance, statements such as "I would make certain that I would prohibit members of this group (Palestinians) from voting or participating in the Lebanese political system" might have had more significant effect on perceptions. Another factor would be an index of how xenophobic some communities are *vis-à-vis* others, as minorities tend to be. For example, it may be that some groups are more xenophobic and hence more susceptible to expressing their prejudices. This may be a better explanation than communication in the case of Shi'ites for instance, who are the ones to have interacted the most with Palestinians.

The role of communication

Regression analysis delineated the importance of increased communication in relation to favorable perceptions of Palestinians. However, there is unequivocal theoretical support for the feasibility of communication in the propagation of pluralistic tendencies and the acceleration of the rise of crosscutting cleavages within societies.

Communication theory used to encourage the optimistic expectation that greater contacts among a state's ethnic groups lead to greater mutual understanding, rather than to greater alienation. However, Rothschild[3] maintains that intensive communication tends to integrate the populations of different geographic regions that belong to the same ethnic group; it does not follow that they have this same effect among different and contrasting ethnic cultures. If the different cultural entities within the political system are dissimilar to the extent whereby they cannot communicate with one another, there develops mutual distrust with no sense of collective identity. For any political structure or system to be workable, it needs a certain minimum of attitudinal commitment on the part of the various communities to work together.

According to Walter Rosenbaum,[4] "a fragmented political culture [as is the case with Lebanon] increases the feeling of isolation and disagreement among social groups, erodes the consensus on political fundamentals and inhibits the development of conditions necessary for a true national community. The prevalence of political distrust between social groups, in fragmented political cultures, is often so endemic that virtually all major groups experience it."

Karl Deutch[5] defines "a sense of community" by analyzing the orientations of one group toward other groups within the state. Lewis Coser[6] stresses that as conflict between groups increases, group members begin to emphasize the differences between the groups rather than focusing on their similarities. An in-group/out-group bias develops and grows more pronounced as conflict increases. This has actually two biases combined: a tendency to favor the in-group; and a tendency to look unfavorably on the out-group and its members, procedures, culture and products.

The history of Lebanon's intercommunal relations is a history characterized by conflict, sectarian independence, low cooperation and minimal social contact. The Lebanese state is composed of several groups whose level of interaction and communication is low.[7] The relations within each sect are superior to the relations between them. The relationship among the sects in Lebanon is restricted to some kind of superficial relations taking the form of social visits.[8] These visits do not develop or show any signs of developing into an organic relationship. Some of the prerequisites for the growth of such a relationship are still lacking, such as the mixed family, common social institutions, common perceptions of pressing problems and solutions and common Lebanese national interests.

As a result of low contacts, mutual feelings of trust and loyalty are also low.[9] Lebanese communities have an inherent fear, which goes back to the nineteenth century or earlier, of massacres, subjugation or marginalization and control. The civil war enhanced these feelings of anxiety, which do not inspire much confidence in the future of intercommunal relations.[10]

The case of the Armenian influx to Lebanon at the beginning of the twentieth century is comparable to the Palestinian situation. However, despite their political neutrality throughout their presence in the country and during the civil war, empirical evidence has shown that not all Lebanese groups perceive Armenians favorably.[11] Having refused to ally themselves during the civil war with Christian rightists, Armenians are not as highly favored by Christian respondents as other Christian groups. Conversely, the cold attitude of Shi'ites and Sunnis toward Armenians is based not on civil war allegiances, but on religion. In a country where anything can tip the sectarian balance, Armenian settlement in the country in 1918 was thought to be, and continues to be seen as, a demographic "weight" in favor of the Christians.

However, the question of the Palestinian presence also differs from Armenian settlement, which occurred long before the establishment of the current system of sectarian power sharing. As soon as a new formula that allocated political power on a confessional basis was reached, it prevented the incorporation of newcomers or even of slight modifications to the system.

The political equation that forms the basis of the Lebanese system

It must be noted that the presence of a power-sharing arrangement characterized by several democratic features[12] has not prevented the eruption of a civil war, as soon sectarian demands were unfullfilled. Daniel Chirot, a sociologist at the University of Washington, has identified five stages of social organization through which a peaceful, integrated society descends into all-out civil war:[13] A necessary condition is that there must be a lack of equal opportunities in the economy; this happens when people feel their ethnic group is competing with another one for limited resources – jobs, food and cultural clout. When people feel threatened by radical change, they seek safety in numbers, and any attack on the group is perceived as a personal affront. Once people are looking through this lens, a crisis is all that is needed to spark an ethnic war.

More often, the crisis is political – a shift in the balance of power between groups that makes both sides nervous. A study that attempted to tie outbreaks of violence in Northern Ireland to the ups and downs of its economy, for example, found no connection between the two. Rather, bloodshed invariably followed changes in the power relationship between Protestants and Catholics. Ethnic conflict is most likely to occur, Chirot concludes, "when people believe that the other group is going to take power away from them, and that they'll be the long-term losers, in every way: culturally, politically, economically." Echoing Chirot, the importance and weight that the Palestinian factor can impose on Lebanon should not be underestimated.

A principal goal of this study has been to assess the impact of social variables on Lebanese communal closeness/hostility to Palestinian using multivariate analysis. The results are clear and consistent. Communication is a significant predictor of attitudes toward resettlement. Specifically, level of communication is inversely and consistently associated with unfavorable perceptions of Palestinian in Lebanon. Therefore, in order to promote refugee integration into Lebanon's social system, communication with this group should be improved. This variable should be taken seriously by Lebanese politicians and policy-makers if the integration of refugees is a possible alternative.

Notes

1 This scale is adopted from Bogardus who introduced the Social Distance Scale for use as an index of the social distance that respondents perceive between themselves and members of different groups defined by nationality, ethnicity, religion, or politics. The scale, or some form of it, has been used in studies involving a variety of populations, including ethnic minorities and has been considered a measure of prejudice. The survey contained a battery of Likert scale questions (responded to in terms of strong agreement, agreement, etc.), tapping various aspects of the preferred social distance between oneself or one's family and Palestinians living in Lebanon. Some items were phrased positively (i.e., indicating tolerance) and others were phrased negatively (i.e., indicating prejudice). From seven of the questions used in the survey, this scale, which assesses respondents' willingness to accept Palestinians in various roles (as a neighbor, friend, etc.) was constructed and checked by various empirical analyses (internal consistency of items in a scale, factor analysis of items and scale inter-correlations). The sum score of the items divided by their number was taken as an indication of negativeness or prejudice. See E. S. Bogardus, "Measuring Social Distance," *Journal of Applied Sociology* 9, pp. 299–308; *A Forty-Year Racial Distance Study*, (Pasadena: University of Southern California Press, 1967); John Fagan, and Michael O'Neill, "A Comparison of Social-Distance Scores Among College-Student Samples," *The Journal of Social Psychology* 66(2) (1965), pp. 281–90; Michael Payne, Jr., Charles York, and John Fagan "Changes in Measured Social Distance Over Time," *Sociometry*, 37(2) (1974), pp. 131–6; Philip Kunz, and Yvonne Ohenebra-Sakyi, "Social Distance: A study of changing views of young Mormons toward black individuals," *Psychological Reports* 65(1) (1989), pp. 195–200; W. E. Lambert and D. M. Taylor, *Coping with Cultural and Racial Diversity in Urban America* (New York: Praeger, 1990).
2 Khashan, "The Despairing Palestinians."
3 Joseph Rothschild, *Ethnopolitics: A conceptual framework* (New York: Columbia University Press, 1981).
4 Walter Rosenbaum, *Political Culture* (New York: Praeger, 1975), p. 37.
5 Karl Deutsch, "Social Mobilization and Political Development," *American Political Science Review* 55 (September 1961), p. 49.
6 Lewis Coser, *The Functions of Social Conflict* (New York: Free Press, 1956).
7 Edward E. Azar, "Lebanon and its Political Culture: Conflict and integration

in Lebanon," in E. A. Azar (eds.), *The Emergence of a New Lebanon: Fantasy or reality?* (New York: Praeger, 1984), p. 40.
8. A. Ghossein, "Geography in the Study of the Lebanese Structure and Crisis," *Haliyyat*, 25 (1982), p. 25.
9. Michael C. Hudson, *The Precarious Republic: Political modernization in Lebanon* (New York: Random House, 1968), p. 34.
10. E. Azar, "Lebanon and its Political Culture," p. 40.
11. See: Hilal Khashan, *Inside the Lebanese Confessional Mind* (Lanham: University Press of America, 1992) and Simon Haddad, "Christian–Muslim Relations and Attitudes toward the Lebanese State," *Journal of Muslim Minority Affairs* 21(1) (April 2001), pp. 131–48.
12. Issam Sleiman, "Equilibre Confessionnel et Equilibre Institutionnel au Liban", in F. Kiwan (eds.), *Le Liban D'aujourd'Hui* (Paris: Cermoccurs Editions, 1994), p. 73: Joseph Maila, "The Ta'if Accord: An evaluation," in Deidre Collings (ed.), *Peace For Lebanon: From war to reconstruction* (New York: Lynne Rienner Publishers, 1994), pp. 31–2.
13. Annie Murphy Paul, "Psychology's Own Peace Corps: Global ethnic conflict," *Psychology Today* 31(4) (July–August, 1998), p.56.

11

Palestinian Refugees' Socio-Political Attitudes in Lebanon

Analysis in previous chapters has focused on: basic Lebanese political attitudes toward Palestinians; the nature and intensity of Lebanese–Palestinian inter-group relations and perceptions; and, Lebanese views toward the permanent settlement of Palestinians in the country. In this chapter, analysis will shift to Palestinian sources of frustration which have direct impact on their situation in Lebanon's refugee camps and within the context of the Arab–Israeli peace process. In order to examine Palestinian refugee's sources of grievances, the following variables were considered:

1. Political allegiance.
2. Socio-economic satisfaction.
3. Palestinian statehood.
4. Likelihood of just peace.
5. Intensity of Palestinian-ness (Palestinian nationalism).
6. Manifestation of radicalism.
7. Voice amenability to permanent settlement outside the Palestinian Authority.

Breaking with the PLO

Since the early 1970s, the PLO has been widely acknowledged as the sole legitimate voice of the Palestinian people. However, in responding to a question on the group in which the respondents vested their allegiance (table 11.1), the PLO received only 19 percent of total responses. In fact, local Islamic groups that first appeared as late as the 1980s surpassed the PLO. Another interesting finding reflected in table 11.1 is that a preference for "none of the above" is widespread; a response that appears to reflect a defection from Arafat's Fatah faction, rather than from opposition factions.

Table 11.1 Political allegiance

	Number	Percentage
PLO	51	19
Pro-Syrian Palestinian groups	20	7
Islamic groups	57	21
Other Palestinian groups	5	2
None	140	51
Total	273	100

In an attempt to explain the decline of the PLO, several political and military developments must be examined. First, the split that occurred within Fatah in 1983, and then the 1985–7 war launched by Lebanese Amal militia against the Palestinian camps in Beirut and southern Lebanon in 1985. These events have altered the politico-military balance that was in order inside refugee camps of Lebanon. Pro-Arafat Fatah forces were redeployed to Southern Lebanon located camps, and while all Palestinian groups maintained a political presence inside the camps, the weight of the PLO was severely reduced (see pp. 30–7).

Second, the vacuum left by a combination of Fatah's focus on activities in the Palestinian Authority and the decision of other secular groups to give priority to political over military action has given unprecedented opportunity for Islamist groups to gain support in the camps. On the other hand, the fostering of improved relations between Islamic groups like Hamas, Islamic Jihad and Hizbullah dramatically increased the groups' penetration of the camps, expanding their influence and ability to mobilize there.[1]

Third, fluctuations in the peace negotiations, as well as more general criticism of Palestinian leadership, appear to have had some effect on the support enjoyed by Fatah and Arafat. Although Arafat gained popularity because he challenged Israel on the issue of Jerusalem, progress toward Palestinian statehood has been completely suspended, in contrast to Palestinians' anticipations when the 1993 Oslo Accords were signed. A Palestinian refugee in the Shatila camp remarked: "I no longer trust the PLO to address our basic needs as a people without a state . . . our own leaders have sacrificed our right for return for autonomy. We feel forgotten and abandoned."[2]

Add to this the mounting opposition to the power exerted by the Palestinian Authority that Arafat heads; all of this, apparently, has reduced the level of support for Palestine's dominant political faction. However, Arafat's ability to provide refugees with regular financial assistance does not appear to compensate for several years of difficulty and disappointment.[3] A majority of respondents seem convinced, at least based on available results, that Fatah and Arafat have little to offer in terms of achieving their political objectives.

Socio-economic conditions

The Palestinian refugees' situation in Lebanon is unique in the region in the degree of political, economic and social exclusion. Poor living and housing conditions, coupled with extremely high rates of unemployment and little access to government education, health and social services, makes these refugees some of the most disadvantaged in the Palestinian diaspora.[4] Clearly therefore, the overwhelming majority of the respondents score low on the socio-economic satisfaction items as table 11.2 demonstrates.

Table 11.2 Socio-economic satisfaction items

Are you satisfied with your personal economic condition?

	Number	Percentage
Yes	4	2
No	248	92
Unsure	19	7
Total	271	101*

I am satisfied with my current life conditions

	Number	Percentage
Yes	7	3
No	262	97
Total	269	100

The Lebanese government has made every effort to make life uncomfortable, and Lebanon unwelcoming, for the Palestinian community.[5] Moreover, Palestinians are regarded neither as nationals nor foreigners but simply as "non-nationals." A harsh policy referred to as "strangulation" of Palestinians is accomplished by extremely restrictive options that provide for employment only by permit and the near-total absence of social welfare provisions[6]. Obtaining a work permit remains a complex and lengthy process that offers neither social security nor insurance benefits nor a regular wage increase, and becomes invalid when its holder is laid off the job. Moreover, employment in large institutions is largely closed to Palestinians because it is governed by sectarian rules. Lebanese labor law states that non-Lebanese must obtain work permits for all regular jobs: construction, sanitation and agriculture. A second law restricts the practice of most professions – medicine, engineering, pharmacy – to Lebanese, forcing Palestinians to take jobs that offer low wages, insecurity and no benefits. Palestinians, however, explicitly are forbidden to work in more than 70 qualified professions, such as medicine and law. These restrictions force them to work in the informal sector with low wages, insecurity and no benefits.[7] In 2000, only 350 work permits were issued to Palestinians.

In post-war Lebanon, Palestinian refugees describe their lives in terms of abnormality. Aside from shortages of shelter, food, safety and access to medical care and education, they have constant doubts about the security of residence. In fact, not only were Palestinians landscaped out of Palestine, but also the erasure continues in exile. A Palestinian lawyer, echoing popular sentiment, has written, "That there are those who believe that the group known as Palestinian refugees in Lebanon will stop existing within a few years."[8]

Palestinian statehood and refugee return

For more than 50 years, Palestinian refugees in Lebanon have faced mounting problems and international neglect, and never more than now, as the humanitarian crisis in the West Bank, East Jerusalem and Gaza diverts attention from their plight. Palestinian fears and concerns have been on the rise, especially since the eruption of the second Intifada and the collapse of the peace negotiations.

Table 11.3 Likelihood of a Palestinian state

Peace negotiations will lead to the establishment of a Palestinian state

	Number	Percentage
Yes	42	16
No	179	66
Unsure	50	19
Total	271	101

I support establishing a Palestinian state even if refugee return is not guaranteed

	Number	Percentage
Yes	68	25
No	201	75
Total	269	100

The peace process will ensure Palestinian refugees' return

	Number	Percentage
Yes	18	7
No	235	86
Unsure	20	7
Total	273	100

Where the breakdown of the peace process apparently has had an impact, understandably, is on expectations and assessments. The poll reported (table 11.3) that only 16 percent of the respondents "expect the current peace process to lead to the establishment of a Palestinian state in the West Bank and Gaza in the coming years." Another 25 percent believe this will not occur if the right of return is not ascertained. In the eyes of the majority, the likelihood of return does not exceed 7 percent. Neither do Palestinian respondents apparently believe that the Israeli government is sincere in its intentions to reach a peaceful resolution to the conflict.

Whereas progress toward peace has been decidedly disappointing from the Palestinian point of view, especially since the 1996 Israeli elections, this has not brought increased opposition to the kind of two-state solution that the PLO has officially championed for at least a decade. Throughout the negotiating process, the issue of the refugees has been and is still encountering formidable forms of resistance from Israeli decision-makers. The Israelis are subjecting the return of the refugees to a barrage of ideological and political objections, both at the public level and in the media. The return of the refugees is being portrayed as a security issue within Israel, and as a prelude to a subtle scheme to undermine the Jewish character of the state, even when it entails only the return of refugees to the areas under Palestinian control.[9]

Expectations and assessments are to at least some degree shaped by events on the ground. Palestinian skepticism runs deep, being pronounced not only before, but also after, Ariel Sharon took power. According to Khashan, "In a single stroke of abrasive behavior Ariel Sharon, Israel's ill-famed personality, has undone seven years of painfully slow progress toward peace between Arabs and Israelis."[10]

Conversely, seen from the Israeli perspective, "pressing for a right of return means prolonging the conflict and perpetuating the misery of the Palestinians . . . a Palestinian state is achievable only in the West Bank and Gaza . . . otherwise, Palestinian statehood will remain an unfulfilled aspiration."[11] It remains to be seen whether the deadlock in the Israeli–Palestinian peace process will be broken, and how Palestinians will respond to continuing stalemate or to a breakthrough.

Likelihood of a just peace

Table 11.4 Perception of a just peace

I believe the Israelis genuinely want peace

	Number	Percentage
Yes	13	5
No	231	85
Unsure	28	10
Total	272	100

I believe the Arabs would provide assistance for the Palestinians

	Number	Percentage
Yes	8	3
No	260	95
Unsure	5	2
Total	273	100

The US is an impartial arbiter in the peace negotiations

	Number	Percentage
Yes	37	14
No	225	82
Unsure	11	4
Total	273	100

When the respondents were asked to assess the role of the US in mediating the peace talks between Arabs and Israelis, only 14 percent said the US performs as an honest broker (table 11.4).

Israel's long-term security requires a stable peace with its neighbors. Given continued American military and technological support, conventional Israeli security is more easily assured today. The greater current threat to Israel comes from regional instability that breeds terrorism and low-level conflict, and from unconventional capabilities that can best be controlled through negotiated incentives in an environment of peace. Clearly, the broader the peace coalition, the easier it will be to confront those who remain outside of it. However, this does not seem to be the view of most respondents, the majority of whom (85%) are skeptical of Israeli peace intentions.

The Oslo Accords enabled Jordan to sign a peace treaty with Israel, led to negotiations between Israel and Syria and emboldened Arab states in the

Gulf and North Africa to forge closer ties with Israel. The deadlock in the peace process since the second Intifada began has halted further normalization of relations between Israel and the Arab world and has intensified opposition to normalization by the general Arab public and its intellectual elites, putting strains even on the peace agreements with Egypt and Jordan. Nevertheless, a mere 3% are convinced of the effectiveness of Arab actions in deterring Israel or even boosting the Palestinian side in their confrontation with Israel. Reflecting the views of refugees in Lebanon, a Munir Maqdah statement, commenting on the Arab Peace Initiative launched at the 2002 Beirut Arab Summit, stated: "All Arabs are traitors . . . they should support the Palestinians and the Intifada. There have been many summits, and nothing ever came out of them. It will be the same this year."

Intensity of "Palestinian-ness"

Have the Palestinians of the camps abandoned the struggle for Palestine and given way to despair? Table 11.5 translates the intensity of Palestinian-ness among respondents who scored high on all three items, suggesting that "Palestinian-ness" is more than a transient trend. This Palestinian nationalism took shape after Palestinian refugees decided to take the issue of ending their displacement into their own hands. Up until the 1967 war, they had fully entrusted the task to Arab states neighboring Israel, especially Nasser's Egypt. But the crushing defeat of Arab armies in 1967 impelled Palestinians to assume full responsibility for their national cause. The Palestine Liberation Organization and Arafat's Fatah Movement, two key Palestinian movements that came to the fore before the 1967 war, in addition to smaller groups such as the Popular Front for the Liberation of Palestine, galvanized the refugees into a national movement.

The battle of Karameh in March 1968, in which Israeli troops for the first time left some of their dead and destroyed equipment behind, served as the focal point in igniting Palestinian nationalism under the leadership of Arafat, who united all 14 Palestinian groups into an umbrella organization under the leadership of the PLO.

The PLO's eviction from Lebanon in 1982 did not weaken Palestinian nationalism. Reuben Slonim, in his investigation of the dire situation of the camps in the aftermath of the 1982 Israeli invasion of Lebanon, reported that Palestinians insist "on having a say in their destiny and carving out that destiny with a gun."[12]

The 1987 Intifada brought a new surge in Palestinian determination to achieve statehood. In 1995 a qualitative survey conducted among the refugees in Lebanon showed that Palestinian desire for statehood remained unchanged, as revealed by the following testimonies: "There are a lot of us who have been deprived of the word 'papa,'" said one young child. "If there were someone to look after the families of martyrs, daughters would have offered their lives, too," added the boy's mother.[13]

Table 11.5   Intensity of Palestinian-ness items

Victory is not worth the sacrifices and losses my people would suffer

	Number	Percentage
Yes	68	25
No	120	68
Unsure	19	7
Total	272	100

We must not be concerned about bloodletting if it achieves our political objectives

	Number	Percentage
Yes	120	46
No	127	49
Unsure	17	6
Total	264	100

I believe that the sanctity of human life in its absolute form is more important than political values

	Number	Percentage
Yes	173	66
No	73	28
Unsure	18	7
Total	264	101

This national sentiment received a major boost after the eruption of the second Intifada in 2000.

Support for impulsive radicalism

When asked to record whether they approved of recourse to militancy in order to attract attention to their plight and regain their rights, a most serious finding was detected (table 11.6). Calls for the reintroduction of guerrilla-type raids against Israel are significant, with almost six of every ten respondents endorsing them; yet, this finding is predictable in view of the fact that terror raids were widely practiced in the past.

Refugees' Socio-Political Attitudes in Lebanon

Table 11.6 Manifestation of radicalism

What is your position regarding peace with the Jewish state?

	Number	Percentage
Support	77	29
Oppose	191	71
Unsure	0	0
Total	268	100

In view of the political climate in the occupied territories, do you believe that the Palestinians in Lebanon should:
Accelerate anti-Israeli operations departing from Lebanon in order to ascertain Palestinian right of return?

	Number	Percentage
Yes	151	56
No	120	44
Unsure	0	0
Total	271	100

Carry out anti-civilian activities (terrorist, suicide attacks) departing from Lebanon in order to ascertain the right of return?

	Number	Percentage
Yes	146	54
No	78	29
Unsure	48	18
Total	272	100

One problem is that radical Palestinians may want to carry the war south using Hizbullah's example as a way of liberating territory from Israel. Thus far, direct attacks across the border with Israel have been few and mostly prevented. But in the present vacuum, observers note that there are 10,000 armed Palestinian guerrillas inside the country who represent serious opposition to the peace process. The fear is that these guerrillas, acting on orders from Arafat, the Syrians, Hizbullah – or out of their own desperation to bring international attention to the refugees' plight – will join the Intifada by staging operations against northern Israel.[14]

Palestinian rejectionist organizations may be authorized by Hizbullah, which jealously guards its monopoly of anti-Israeli activity, to conduct attacks from Lebanon. This follows repeated rhetoric by Hizbullah officials in support of the Palestinian uprising and increased motivation by veteran Palestinian groups to get into the action. It would not be the first time Hizbullah is thought to have made use of willing Palestinians.[15]

Amenability to permanent settlement outside Palestine

Are the preceding results enough to suggest that Palestinian frustration with their economic conditions, the peace process and support for impulsive radicalism will be enough to make them abandon the right of return? The reports from the various camps seem to concur, as can be gathered from the responses detailed in table 11.7.

Table 11.7 Probing alternatives for resolving the Palestinian problem

Would you accept Lebanese citizenship?

	Number	Percentage
Yes	51	19
No	155	57
Unsure	64	24
Total	270	100

Would you accept permanent settlement in Lebanon?

	Number	Percentage
Yes	41	15
No	214	79
Unsure	17	6
Total	272	100

Would you accept leaving Lebanon for a third country other than Palestine?

	Number	Percentage
Yes	71	26
No	123	45
Unsure	78	29
Total	272	101

Would you accept permanent settlement in oil-rich Arab states?

	Number	Percentage
Yes	57	21
No	164	64
Unsure	41	15
Total	272	101[1]

Would you accept permanent settlement in a Western country?

	Number	Percentage
Yes	68	25
No	131	48
Unsure	72	27
Total	27	101

The respondents voiced qualified opposition for permanent residence outside Palestine. A majority of 79 percent and 57 percent, respectively, rejected the avenue of permanent residence and citizenship. Insisting on the refugees' right of return, Brigadier Sultan Abul-Aynayn, the Palestine Authority representative in Lebanon, stipulated: "I have not fought 30 years of my life to stay here . . . Although I love Lebanon, why should I take up Lebanese nationality? If one hundred thousand Palestinians are made to stay here, I can't guarantee they won't fight their way out."[16]

In view of the current socio-economic and political climate in the country, Palestinian respondents' preferences are not surprising. However, their outright rejection of resettlement in other countries (65%), namely oil-rich Arab countries, deserves attention. In the absence of democracy in the Arab world and with the continuation of an inegalitarian economic order, Arab governments' tolerance of Palestinians has declined over time, particularly after the Gulf War. Citizenship and residency rights have been denied to Palestinian refugees everywhere in the Arab world except Jordan, the initial rationale being solidarity and the affirmation of the Palestinians' right to return to their homeland.[17]

However, Palestinian lack of enthusiasm for relocation to Western countries is also explained in relation to political and social factors. On the one hand, media reports of a Canadian proposal for taking in several thousand Palestinians as part of the Arab–Israeli negotiations has made an impact. Palestinian respondents appear aware of these supposed efforts and widely reject such plans, possibly fearing that this may contribute to an abandonment of the right of return.[18] On another level, Palestinian migration to European countries has also had little success. Those who have attempted to settle there have been faced with legal and social obstacles. Naturally, individual experiences have been reported to the wider refugee population.[19] The plight of the Palestinians is roughly contemporary to that of the Arab–Israeli conflict and remains a core requirement for peace in the area. The Palestinian refugees are not ready to be absorbed in Arab states, nor do they want to be relocated to Western countries. They would prefer to hang on to the right of return, which they believe will eventually lead to repatriation. A major factor behind their opposition to settlement lies in a high level of radicalism and commitment to the continuation of the struggle against Israel.

Domestically, Palestinians in Lebanon have endured military occupation, deportation, torture, land confiscation, massacres, siege, aerial bombardments and internecine conflict in Lebanon. But all this has been unable to break their determination. On a regional level, the austere political atmosphere currently reigns in the Middle East, coupled with the breakdown of the peace process and the likelihood of an American assault against Iraq, further complicates the refugees' situation. And while Lebanon's Palestinian community continues to be worried about its fate, it can only hope for a better treatment by the Lebanese authorities and more sympathetic gestures by the public.

Notes
1   Nicole Brackman, "Palestinian Refugees in Lebanon: New source of cross-border tension," *The Washington Institute's Peace Watch*, 263 (May 30, 2000).
2   Stephen J. Sosebee, "Progress toward Statehood Tightens Noose around Palestinians in Lebanon," *Washington Report on Middle East Affairs*, (February/March 1996), p. 22.
3   Rosemary Sayyigh, "Palestinians in Lebanon: Pawns on a tilted chessboard," www.between-lines.org/archives, June 2001.
4   See, for example, Steven Edminster, *Trapped on All Sides: The marginalization of Palestinian refugees in Lebanon* (Washington, D.C.: US Committee for Refugees, 1999); Mahmoud Abbas, "The Socio-Economic Conditions of the Palestinians in Lebanon: The housing situation of the Palestinians in Lebanon," *Journal of Refugee Studies* 10(3), pp. 380–1; Wadie Said, "The Palestinians in Lebanon: The rights of the victims of the Palestinian–Israeli peace process," *Columbia Human Rights Law Review* 30(2) (Spring 1999), pp. 315–57.
5   Suheil Al-Natour, "The Legal Status of Palestinians in Lebanon." Paper presented to the to the CLS/RSP conference on the Palestinians in Lebanon. (Oxford, September, 1996).
6   Julie Peteet, "Lebanon: Palestinian refugees in the post-war period," http://www.en.monde-diplomatique.fr/focus/mideast/region-lebanon-refugee (December 1999).

7   A study by the Norwegian-based Fafo Institute for Applied Social Science concluded that only 42 percent of refugees' population have a job, most of whom are men who engage in trade, manufacturing and construaction work. Eighty per cent considered local work and business opportunities very bad. See Khalil Zayan, "Norwegian NGO releases report on dire condition of Palestinian refugees," *Daily Star*, Beirut, April 7, 2000.
8   Suheil Al-Natour, "The Legal Status of Palestinian Refugees in Lebanon," in Refugees in the Middle East, Nordic NGO Seminar (Oslo: Norwegian Refugee Council, March 26–27, 1993).
9   Hussein Agha and Robert Malley, "A solution is possible now, Middle East Peace negotiations have failed. But the US can make a final deal stick," *The Guardian,* Friday, March 29, 2002.
10 Hilal Khashan, "An Intifada for Peace and Against its Process," *The Arab World Geographer* 3(3) (Fall 2000), pp.157–8.
11 Leonard Cole, "A Palestinian Return to Nowhere," *Midstream*, 47(6) (2000), pp. 9–13.
12 Reuben Slonim, "Palestinian Refugee Camps Breed Future Threat to Israel," *Journal of Palestine Studies* 12(2) (1983), pp. 194–6.
13 Abd al-Salam Aql, "Palestinian Refugees of Lebanon Speak," *Journal of Palestine Studies* 25(1) (1995), pp. 54–5.
14 Scott Macleod, "Can't Go Home Again: For Palestinians in Lebanon, life is hard and the prospect of return is fading by the day," *Time International*, 157 (12) (March 26, 2001), p. 229.
15 A demonstration by Palestinians bussed from Beirut to a border gate near Ramieh was used as a diversion, allowing Hizbullah to kidnap three Israeli soldiers from the Shebaa Farms in October 2000. Two weeks later, suspected fighters of the Democratic Front for the Liberation of Palestine (DFLP) staged an aborted attempt to cross the border four kilometers east of Ghajar. The operation is believed to have been arranged by Hizbullah to test the response of nearby Israeli troops. The three DFLP fighters picked an exposed area, opposite the Israeli Army's Abbassieh outpost and one of the few stretches of the border where the new hi-tech security fence had been built. The fighters were swiftly detected and intercepted by Israeli troops. Two of the DFLP fighters were killed, and the third escaped wounded. That was the last operation staged by Palestinians.
16 Nicholas Blanford, "Fatah Chief: Beirut Asked for Help," *The Daily Star*, November 16, 1999.
17 Abbas Shiblak, "Residency Status and Civil Rights of Palestinians in Host Arab States," *Journal of Palestine Studies* 25(3) (1996), pp. 36–45.
18 Claire Chokr, "Canada wadaat mashruan tawtinian aradatho ala almutaadidat alataraf wa lijan minal muthakafin alfilistiniyyn tataharak dakhilian khawfan alal masir" (Canada has set a resettlement scheme and presented it to the multilateral working group; committees of Palestinian intellectuals started a local activity fearing about their future), *An-Nahar*, March 14, 2000.
19 Hussein Chaaban, "Palestinians Emigrants from Lebanon," *An-Nahar*, July 23, 2001.

Conclusion
Toward a National Consensus?

The survey results have shown that talk of permanently settling Palestinian refugees in Lebanon triggers wide public opposition and may pose a threat to the country's security and political stability.

Although not all Lebanese factions consented to the 1989 Ta'if Accord, the deal nevertheless marked a turning point in the civil war and managed to re-establish a modicum of security in the country. As a result, Lebanon moved into a reconstruction phase. Resettling the Palestinians would invite more Sunni political demands that would threaten Shi'ite gains accorded by Ta'if and also threaten to further undermine Maronite power. The unwillingness of all Lebanese groups to return to the trauma of civil war, along with hopes for a better future and worries of what the future might hold, seem to unify the Lebanese in opposition to permanent Palestinian settlement.

Equally, however, the memory of the civil war might also explain why only a minority is prepared to resist militarily if settlement were to be imposed on the country. The study also shows that, more than any other group, Druze and Sunni respondents are ready to accept settlement. This is noteworthy because settlement has long been seen by many Sunnis – traditionally strong advocates of Arab nationalism – as an admission of final defeat by Israel. Not all of them appear ready to accept the loss of an Arab cause that is linked to the repatriation of the refugees.

Although part of these findings is to be expected – most notably in the case of Christian groups – those related to Muslim groups are surprising and interesting. They are also at variance with the arguments advanced by some scholars, to the effect that *"tawtin"* or resettlement, is probably the only issue on which the views of the Lebanese – across all ideological and confessional lines – agree. This argument is presented by Khazen,[1] who contends that the Palestinian presence, from being the most divisive issue in post-independence Lebanese politics, is also one of the few issues that also arouses national consensus in post-war Lebanon.

A more plausible argument is offered by Sayyigh,[2] who asserts that the

Conclusion: Toward a National Consensus?

Lebanese public can be divided into three main segments: (1) a determined anti-Palestinian minority; (2) a large component that is indifferent to the Palestinian issue unless aroused by sectarian campaigning; and (3) a minority that positively supports the refugees.

Findings from the present study lend only partial support to this argument. Tolerance for Palestinians defined in terms of degree of endorsement or rejection of intercommunal ties – social, civic, residential, educational – with Palestinians bears no significant relationship to attitude toward resettlement. Intense anti-Palestinianism is discernible in the case of Christian groups, namely in statements like: "Usually, we don't care about them. Sometimes we feel pity for them because they are poor. But we don't think that they belong here."[3] A reconstructive ethos promoting "Lebanon for the Lebanese," carried by Lebanese Christians throughout the civil war, is reiterinated usually by Christian leaders who tend to exaggerate the size of the Palestinian community and use the question of resettlement to flourish their political vision of partition.[4] Religious affinity also plays a part in this extreme position, since the Palestinian refugee population is nearly all Muslim.[5] Prior to the civil war, in order to add a sectarian gloss to the refugee issue, and in a demographic attempt to bolster the Christian population, the Lebanese government made available Lebanese citizenship to Palestinian Christians.

Beyond political factors, however, such as the deterioration of Palestinian–Lebanese relationship, heavy-handed Israeli retaliation and PLO excesses, a set of economic asymmetries added to Palestinian–Shi'ite antagonism. Both communities lived side by side, but the Shi'ites generally belonged to a lower socio-economic spectrum. Underclass resentment was aroused because of the material advantage enjoyed by Palestinians who were well established in Arab oil-producing states, projecting Palestinians as aliens, intruders and destroyers of "our country."[6] Referring to Palestinian misbehavior during their presence in Lebanon, a Shi'ite villager told Norton: "We gave Palestinians everything and they gave us back insults, corpses and lessons in corruption."[7]

This negative position, however, extended only to a minority of Sunni respondents. Khashan and Palmer, who examined Sunni perceptions during the civil war, found that the dominant position enjoyed by Palestinians during that period, while not vociferously opposed by the Sunnis, was complicated by the fact that Sunni Lebanese generally accorded the Palestinian refugees an inferior social status. Thus, Palestinian–Sunni Lebanese affinity was partially eroded by military dominance of Palestinians and by the reversal of status roles.[8] While some Sunnis tended to distance themselves from Palestinians, this tendency is stronger among less-educated Sunnis than their college-educated counterparts.

Conclusion: Toward a National Consensus?

Indeed, this result is striking since the integration of refugees is supposed to take place, according to experts, within their sub-community. However, this finding is in line with the position adopted by most Sunni politicians. In 1990, even the Sunni Muslim leaders – who theoretically had most to gain from the assimilation of the Sunni Palestinians into Lebanese society – refused to welcome them. This ultimately led to the unexpected amendment to the constitution, refusing non-Lebanese permanent residence in the country. Later, Sunni Prime Minister Rafik Hariri explicitly declared: "Lebanon will never, ever integrate Palestinians. They will not receive civic or economic rights or even work permits. Integration would take the Palestinians off the shoulders of the international agency which has supported them since 1948."[9]

Pro-Palestinian voices present a weak minority in favor of resettlement. A housing project submitted by the Canadian government to help provide a certain measure of relief to the homeless refugees through the construction of new barracks outside Beirut was supported in 1994 by Druze leader Walid Jumblatt, who was at the time minister for refugees. However, the media leaked the talks and the violent protests that ensued led to the abandonment of the entire project. This was a symptom of the fact that any initiative that can be interpreted as indirect assent to the Palestinians remaining is interpreted as a confessionalistic move. The Druze minority was mainly interested in a buffer zone of loyal Palestinians between them and the expanding Shi'ite population. This is a clear indicator of expressed social desirability of Palestinians by a large segment of the Druze community.

Implications for Arab–Israeli Peace

The current Arab–Israeli negotiating process, which began in Madrid in 1991, addresses the Palestinian issue in two ways, with one track of multilateral talks devoted to the issue of Arab states hosting Palestinians, and another on "final status" negotiations between the Palestinian Authority and the Israelis. But Lebanon fears its own Palestinian population will be neglected in both tracks. First, it has no presence in talks between Israel and Syria, and second, it is absent from the multilateral talks' Refugee Working Group, chaired by Canada. Moreover, since former Israeli Prime Minister Ehud Barak ruled out the return of hundreds of thousands of refugees to Israel, Lebanon has also withdrawn from the bilateral talks between itself and the Jewish state.

For Israel, however, whatever the legal and moral merit of the Arab claims of the "right of return," this will not under any conceivable set of circumstances be realized. No Israeli government will ever agree to substantially change the demographic balance of the Jewish state, since the state's very *raison d'être* is its Jewish character. Former Israeli Prime Minister Shimon Peres has voiced the Israeli position on this point:

> a maximalist claim; if accepted, it would wipe out the national character of the state of Israel, making the Jewish majority into a minority. Consequently, there is no chance it will be accepted, either now or in the future.[10]

By the same token, Maronite Christian opposition to Palestinian settlement in Lebanon is openly expressed by the Maronite patriarch, Cardinal Nasrallah Sfeir, on the basis that it will tip the country's delicate sectarian balance:

> the peace that is being promised may have adverse consequences. If the resettlement of Palestinians in vast underpopulated Arab countries is not acceptable, then the effect on a small, overpopulated country like Lebanon would be even more dire.[11]

In line with these popular attitudes, Lebanese officials continue to refuse settlement and to insist on repatriation. Even as Israel has refused even to consider repatriation, Lebanon has made resolving the refugee situation a precondition for peace. If the present attitudes hold, they will constitute an obstacle to the US-brokered negotiations between the Arabs and Israel.

Obstacles to Settlement?

Because Lebanon suffers from economic stagnation, a plausible explanation is sometimes advanced that perception of economic insecurity is directly related to opposition to resettlement.[12] The economic dimension is particularly worthy of examination, as Lebanon may be expected to accept permanent settlement of refugees, if it is induced by a tremendous aid/development package. If economic conditions improve as a result of Palestinian resettlement, would this reduce social distance and hence opposition for resettlement?[13] President Lahoud is quoted saying: "We have received an international offer of $20 billion to settle the Palestinian refugees living on our territory. This figure is close to Lebanon's public debt, which is an important factor of the pressures that are being exerted on us."[14]

Judgments about the perceived consequences and economic needs in particular appear to be important in determining the attitude toward resettlement. This proposition, which receives support from findings about the importance of the nature of perception of immigration on economic status, offers a promising area for future research.

Conclusion: Toward a National Consensus?

Keeping in mind that the nature of the sample employed in the present study may limit the generalizability of the obtained results, the overall findings carry a number of implications for the issues raised on the current debate over Palestinian permanent settlement in Lebanon, and also for the Lebanese system as a whole. How genuine are Lebanese fears about resettlement? Palestinian "otherness" is juxtaposed not to a homogeneous singular category of Lebanese, but to a shifting set of sectarian groups and alliances, each with its own particular interests and fears. A majority of Christian and Shi'ite respondents display intense prejudice toward Palestinians, suggesting the presence of social barriers that hinder socio-economic integration of camp inhabitants and their children.

On the other hand, the results also suggest the presence of a structural weakness in the Lebanese system. Lebanese scholar Joseph Maila concedes that the permanent settlement of the Palestinian refugees in Lebanon could upset Lebanon's social mosaic.

The kind of linkage between the Palestinians and the Palestinian Authority is likely to create problems for the Lebanese in the coming years.[15] Hence, for most Lebanese the question is about their own political survival, not Palestinian resettlement. These negative attitudes, coupled with further government restrictions and pressures on Palestinians, imply that permanent settlement is a dangerous alternative for it threatens the regime with collapse.

Malik[16] maintains that Lebanon cannot absorb so many Palestinians and remain stable. However, many Palestinians were naturalized under the 1994 naturalization decree. The only conceivable way the rest – or even some – of these Palestinians can be accepted as Lebanese without creating an uproar is if the affected communities (mainly the Shi'ites and the Christians) can be compensated politically through constitutionally grounded guarantees that preserve individual and communal rights for all, regardless of demographic fluctuations: In other words, by legislating safeguards that protect Lebanon's pluralistic character and consensus political arrangement.

If the actual perceptions stand, resettlement will create a potential for communal conflict and will affect the social cohesion of the society. In connection with this, the Lebanese government finds itself compelled to consent to a continuing Palestinian military presence in refugee camps, something that threatens to reignite the civil war.

Moreover, refugees in Palestinian camps have grown increasingly restive over the course of the current Intifada. Fears that the fighting in the Palestinian territories could spark a series of organized cross-border attacks into Israel from south Lebanon are being discounted by Lebanese authorities. Muslim clerics, however, have been calling for active support to liberate Palestine, and Christians have responded by condemning "the

Conclusion: Toward a National Consensus?

voices announcing their intentions to violate Lebanese laws and attempt to go back to a past that the Lebanese want to forget."[17]

Furthermore, Lebanese authorities cannot dismiss the potential of friction with Palestinian groups who might attempt to use Lebanese territory to instigate attacks on Israel in view of deteriorating Israeli–Palestinian relations. This would be reminiscent of events leading to the 1978 and 1982 Israeli incursions into Lebanon. Lebanese President Emile Lahoud has called for international peacekeeping troops to help disarm Palestinian camps – an unfulfilled request that does not bode well for future security conditions in Lebanon short of a comprehensive Arab–Israeli peace agreement.[18]

The situation is further complicated in light of the breakdown of Syrian –Israeli talks. Syria, which exercises full hegemony over Lebanese public life and political decision-making, supports the maintaining of a Palestinian armed presence as part of its strategy. Undoubtedly, the Syrians would choose to reactivate the Lebanese–Israeli front, in the event of the failure of the peace talks, through their pro-Syrian Palestinian fighters in the camps.

Thus, Lebanon remains a fragile body politic in the aftermath of its civil war, and the Lebanese are deeply divided on how to handle a host of national security issues, including the question of Palestinian refugees. The divisions among the Lebanese on this question are increasing, and there is a high probability that the appalling humanitarian and political situation of the Palestinian refugees in Lebanon may reignite armed conflict between Arabs and Israelis.

The international community may eventually require Lebanon to take a step toward resettling Palestinian refugees, namely by easing official restrictions, whenever solving the issue of the refugees becomes necessary. Both France and the US have advised Lebanese officials to cease their public statements on the resettlement of the refugees and to take a more logical stand in order to find a real solution for this long standing humanitarian and security problem. Accordingly, the Palestinian refugee issue cannot be resolved outside the bilateral talks between Lebanon and Israel, and without the intervention of great powers. "Insisting on refusing resettlement is not a practical solution. The Palestinians will not be repatriated, but this doesn't mean they will be nationalized; other alternatives will be considered."[19] As revealed by this study, granting Palestinians some form of civil rights, such as the right to work, is welcomed by many Muslims. Granting such rights would serve to alleviate Palestinians' socio-economic situation in Lebanon and help ease the country's economic problems. Accordingly, Palestinians would be able to assume the standing of a community in the diaspora, like any other Arab community in Lebanon, and the government would be able to correct the anomalous situation of

Conclusion: Toward a National Consensus?

the Palestinians, with its corresponding restrictions, without considering this step a move toward indirect resettlement.

Notes

1 Farid El-Khazen, "Permanent Settlement of Refugees in Lebanon: A recipe for conflict," *Journal of Refugee Studies* 10(3) (1997).
2 Rosemary Sayyigh, "Palestinian Refugees in Lebanon: Implantation, transfer or return?" *Middle East Policy* 7(1) (2001), pp. 95–105.
3 Ulrich Koltermann, "Who Really Wants Them? Palestinians in Lebanon fed up with being a bargaining chip," *The Jerusalem Times*, June 27, 1997.
4 Maronite politicians such as Michel Edde and Naamatullah Abi-Nasr have claimed that the number of Palestinians in Lebanon is even as high as 500,000 and 600,000 respectively, stressing that resettling them means partitioning the country.
5 Julie Peteet, "Lebanon: Palestinian refugees in the post-war period," http://www.en.monde-diplomatique.fr/focus/mideast/region-lebanon-refugee, (December 1997).
6 Rosemary Sayyigh, *Too Many Enemies*, (1994).
7 Augustus R. Norton, *Amal and The Shi'ites: Struggle for the soul of Lebanon* (Austin, University of Texas Press, 1987).
8 Hilal Khashan and Monte Palmer, "The Economic Basis of Civil Conflict in Lebanon: A survey analysis of Sunnite Muslims," *Journal of Arab Affairs* 1(1) (October 1981), pp.113–33.
9 J. Cooley, "Lebanon Hopes to Join Syrian–Israeli Peace Talks," Center for Polic Analysis on Palestine: www.palestinecenter.org/cpap/pubs/19991214ib.html.
10 Shimon Peres with Arye Naor, *The New Middle East* (New York: Henry Holt, 1993), p. 189.
11 *Al-Hayat*, March. 13, 2000.
12 This dimension receives additional support knowing that that unemployment in Lebanon is said to have exceeded 27 percent and that the demographic composition of Lebanese society includes a formidable percentage (31%) of foreigners. (Source: Debate regarding Palestinian Presence in Lebanon MTV Television, Beirut, November 11, 1999.)
13 There are widespread rumors that Lebanon will be compensated for settling the refugees, enabling it to pay down the debt, which is more than 140 percent of the country's gross domestic product. The $30 billion public debt has mostly accumulated since 1992 to pay for post-civil war reconstruction, a massive bureaucracy and an army and security apparatus. The economic problem has become more acute with debt-servicing alone exceeding government revenues in the first half of the year.
14 *An-Nahar*, August 15, 2000.
15 Interview with Joseph Maila, in *Al-Nahar*, February 25, 2000.
16 Habib Malik, *Between Damascus and Jerusalem: Lebanon and the Middle East peace*. Policy Paper 45, The Washington Institute For Near East Policy (Washington, 2000), p. 44.

Conclusion: Toward a National Consensus?

17 *The Daily Star,* October 10, 2000.
18 N. Blanford and N. Kawas "Lahoud warns UN to prevent mini-wars; President predicts daily violence if camps are not disarmed," *The Daily Star,* Beirut, March 6, 2000.
19 *Al-Dyiar*, September 30, 2000.

Appendix A: Palestinian Resettlement Questionnaire

I Independent Variables

A. Age

1. Age

(a) 18 years to 25 years
(b) 26 years to 33 years
(c) 34 years to 41 years
(d) 42 years to 49 years
(e) 50 years and older

B. Gender

2. Gender

(a) Male   (b) Female

C. Socio-economic situation

3. How do you describe your immediate family's income by Lebanese standards?

(a) High
(b) Above average
(c) Average
(d) Below average
(e) Well below average

4. What is your occupation?

5. In terms of general social classes, would you consider yourself to be a member of the:
(a) Upper class

Appendix A: Resettlement Questionnaire

(b) Middle class
(c) Working class

D. Region of residence

6. In what part of Lebanon do you reside?

(a) Beirut
(b) Southern Mount Lebanon
(c) Northern Mount Lebanon
(d) Beak
(e) South
(f) North

E. Religious sect

7. What is your religious affiliation by birth?

(a) Maronite
(b) Greek-Catholic
(c) Greek-Orthodox
(d) Sunni
(e) Shi'ite
(f) Druze

F. Support for political groups

8. Name the Lebanese political group whose activities you support most?

(a) Right-wing
(b) Leftist
(c) Islamic fundamentalist
(d) Secular
(e) None
(f) Other

G. Blame for war and projection of hostility on Palestinians

9. Do you blame the Palestinians for their role in the Lebanese civil war?

(a) Yes   (b) No

10. If yes, to what extent do you blame them?

(a) Fully
(b) Significantly
(c) Partially

Appendix A: Resettlement Questionnaire

11. In your opinion, the the Lebanese civil war is the responsibility of:

(a) Lebanese parties
(b) Palestinians
(c) Both

12. How close do you feel to Palestinians as a group?

(a) Very close
(b) Close
(c) Distant
(d) Very distant
(e) Neither close nor distant

13. How close do you feel to Sunnis as a group?

(a) Very close
(b) Close
(c) Distant
(d) Very distant
(e) Neither close nor distant

14. How close do you feel to Maronites as a group?

(a) Very close
(b) Close
(c) Distant
(d) Very distant
(e) Neither close nor distant

H. Empathy with Palestinians

15. How often have you felt sympathy for the Palestinians?

(a) Most of the time
(b) Sometimes
(c) Never

16. Can you cite incidents where you have sympathized with them?

J. Position on Palestinian civil rights

17. In your opinion, the 1994 naturalization decree was:

(a) Appropriate
(b) Naturalization should be stopped in the future
(c) The decree should be repealed

Appendix A: Resettlement Questionnaire

18. In your opinion, the major deficiencies of the 1994 naturalization decree were:

(a) granting citizenship to Palestinians
(b) not granting citizenship to Lebanese in the diaspora
(c) threatening Lebanon's interests

19. Do you think Palestinian community of Lebanon should be eligible for?

(a) public education
(b) state welfare
(c) employment
(d) all of the above
(e) none of the above

K. Nature and extent of past contact with Palestinians

20. I have frequent personal contact with Palestinians in the following areas:

(a) residential
(b) civic
(c) friendship
(d) occupational
(e) political
(f) none

21. How comfortable have you felt communicating with Palestinians?

(a) very comfortable
(b) comfortable
(c) not comfortable
(d) not comfortable at all
(e) unsure

L. Tolerance for Palestinians

22. How strongly would you object or support if a member of your family had any relations with Palestinians?

(a) strongly support
(b) support
(c) object
(d) strongly object
(e) unsure

Appendix A: Resettlement Questionnaire

23. Do you think that there should be laws against marriage between Lebanese and Palestinians?

(a) strongly think so
(b) think so
(c) do not think so
(d) strongly do not think so
(e) unsure

24. How would you feel if a relative of yours were planning to marry a Palestinian?

(a) strongly support
(b) support
(c) object
(d) strongly object
(e) unsure

25. Do you think that Lebanese and Palestinian students should go to the same schools?

(a) strongly think so
(b) think so
(c) do not think so
(d) strongly does not think so
(e) unsure

26. Would you support or object to sending your children to schools where Palestinians students are a majority?

(a) strongly support
(b) support
(c) object
(d) strongly object
(e) unsure

27. Would you accept Palestinians living in your neighborhood?

(a) strongly accept
(b) accept
(c) object
(d) strongly object
(e) unsure

Appendix A: Resettlement Questionnaire

28. Would you accept living in a neighborhood where the Palestinians are a majority?

(a) strongly accept
(b) accept
(c) object
(d) strongly object
(e) unsure

29. In your opinion, the Palestinians in Lebanon should be:

(a) granted citizenship
(b) granted immigrant status
(c) resettled outside Lebanon

M. Awareness of resettlement

30. How much info do you have on the "Palestinian resettlement issue?"

(a) very much
(b) some
(c) little
(d) none

31. How important is the "Palestinian resettlement issue" to you?

(a) very much
(b) somewhat
(c) little
(d) not at all

32. Do you think resettlement will be imposed on Lebanon?

(a) strongly think so
(b) think so
(c) do not think so
(d) strongly do not think so
(e) unsure

N. Attitude toward an imposed resettlement

33. If resettlement were imposed, would you:

(a) accept it
(b) reject it
(c) unsure

Appendix A: Resettlement Questionnaire

O. Perceived consequences of resettlement

34. Given your understanding of the issue of Palestinians resettlement, would you say resettlement would have:

(a) positive repercussions
(b) negative repercussions
(c) damaging repercussions
(d) no repercussions

35. In your opinion, what is the nature of the expected negative consequences for resettlement?

(a) sectarian imbalance
(b) economic problems
(c) political problems

36. If resettlement were imposed, would you still accept living under the existing political system (the Ta'if Accord)?

(a) strongly accept
(b) accept
(c) object
(d) strongly object
(e) Unsure

37. If no, what would be the alternative political option?

(a) partition
(b) federation
(c) authoritarian state
(d) religious state
(e) unsure

38. Do you agree with the claim that, as a result of Palestinian resettlement, another civil war will break out?

(a) strongly agree
(b) agree
(c) do not agree
(d) strongly do not agree
(e) unsure

P. Expected course of action to resist resettlement

39. If resettlement were imposed, how likely is it you would actually try to do something to resist it?

(a) very much likely

Appendix A: Resettlement Questionnaire

(b) likely
(c) unlikely
(d) very much unlikely
(e) unsure

40. If resettlement were imposed, I would:

(a) resist it violently
(b) resist it peacefully
(c) acquiesce

41. How much do you think that your actions would be successful in preventing the implementation of resettlement?

(a) strongly think so
(b) think so
(c) do not think so
(d) strongly do not think so
(e) unsure

42. Should, in the future, the strategic situation in the Middle East change, would you then reconsider your position on Palestinian resettlement?

(a) yes
(b) no
(c) unsure

Appendix B: Palestinian Residents in Lebanese Camps Questionnaire

I. Independent Variables

A. Age

1. Age

(a) 18 years to 25 years
(b) 26 years to 33 years
(c) 34 years to 41 years
(d) 42 years to 49 years
(e) 50 years and older

B. Gender

2. Gender

(a) Male
(b) Female

C. Socio-economic situation

3. How do you describe your family's standard by Lebanese standards?

(a) high
(b) above average
(c) average
(d) below average
(e) well below average

4. Level of education:
(a) college
(b) intermediate
(c) elementary
(d) none

Appendix B: Lebanese Camps Questionnaire

5. What is your occupation?

6. Marital status:

(a) married
(b) single
(c) divorced or widowed

D. Support for political groups

7. Name the Palestinian political group whose activities you support most?

(a) Fatah Movement
(b) Popular Front
(c) Hamas
(d) Al-Jihad al-Islami
(e) None
(f) Other

G. Self-esteem

8. Do you feel secure about your immediate family's economic situation?

(a) very secure
(b) secure
(c) insecure
(d) very insecure
(e) uncertain

9. Are you satisfied with your present life?

(a) strongly think so
(b) think so
(c) do not think so
(d) strongly do not think so
(e) uncertain

II. Peace Outlook

A. Faith in Israeli peace intentions

10. Generally speaking, do you believe that the Israelis genuinely want peace with the Palestinians?

(a) strongly believe so
(b) believe so

Appendix B: Lebanese Camps Questionnaire

(c) do not believe so
(d) strongly do not believe so
(e) uncertain

B. Faith in Arab support for Palestinians

11. Do you believe that Arab governments would ever provide meaningful assistance to the Palestinians in their confrontation with Israel?

(a) strongly believe so
(b) believe so
(c) do not believe so
(d) strongly do not believe so
(e) uncertain

C. Faith in American resolve to achieve peace

12. Do you believe in the ability of the US to act as an impartial arbiter between Palestinians and Israel?

(a) strongly believe so
(b) believe so
(c) do not believe so
(d) strongly do not believe so
(e) uncertain

D. Prospects for Palestinian statehood

13. Do you believe that peaceful negotiations will eventually lead to the establishment of a viable Palestinian state?

(a) strongly believe so
(b) believe so
(c) do not believe so
(d) strongly do not believe so
(e) uncertain

14. Would you support the establishment of a Palestinian state even if it does not guarantee the refugees right to return?

(a) strongly support
(b) support
(c) do not support
(d) strongly do not support
(e) uncertain

Appendix B: Lebanese Camps Questionnaire

E. Personal commitment to peace

15. Are you personally committed to peace with Israel as a strategic choice?

(a) strongly committed
(b) committed
(c) not committed
(d) strongly not committed
(e) uncertain

F Refugees' resettlement

16. Do you think that the peace process will ensure the refugees' right to return?

(a) strongly think so
(b) think so
(c) do not think so
(d) strongly do not think so
(e) uncertain

17. Would you accept leaving Lebanon for a third country other than Palestine?

(a) strongly accept
(b) accept
(c) refuse
(d) strongly refuse
(e) uncertain

18. Would you accept resettlement in Lebanon if it serves as a start to solving social problems?

(a) strongly accept
(b) accept
(c) refuse
(d) strongly refuse
(e) uncertain

19. Would you accept Lebanese citizenship?

(a) strongly accept
(b) accept
(c) refuse
(d) strongly refuse
(e) uncertain

Appendix B: Lebanese Camps Questionnaire

20. Would you accept permanent settlement in a Western country?

(a) strongly accept
(b) accept
(c) refuse
(d) strongly refuse
(e) uncertain

21. Would you accept permanent settlement in the Gulf?

(a) strongly accept
(b) accept
(c) refuse
(d) strongly refuse
(e) uncertain

22. If the peace negotiations do not provide for the refugees return to their homeland, would you support the acceleration of anti-Israeli operations?

(a) strongly support
(b) support
(c) oppose
(d) strongly oppose
(e) uncertain

23. If the peace negotiations do not provide for the refugees return to their homeland, would you carry suicide attacks against Israeli targets?

(a) strongly support
(b) support
(c) oppose
(d) strongly oppose
(e) uncertain

Select Bibliography

Mahmoud Abbas, "The Socio-Economic Conditions of the Palestinians in Lebanon: The housing situation of the Palestinians in Lebanon," *Journal of Refugee Studies* 10(3) (1997), pp. 380–1.

Joseph Abou-Khalil, *Kissat al-Mawarina fi al-Harb: Sirat Zatiat* (The History of the Maronites During the Civil War: A biography), (Beirut, Sharikat al-Matbouat li al-Tawsik wa al-Nashr, 1990).

Leslie A. Adelson, "Opposing Oppositions: Turkish–German questions in contemporary German Studies", *German Studies Review* 17(2) (1994), pp. 305–30.

T. Adorno, E. Frenkel-Brunswick, D. Levinson and N. Sanford, *The Authoritarian Personality* (New York: Harper, 1950).

Fouad Ajami, *The Dream Palace of the Arabs* (NewYork: Pantheon Books, 1998).

Susan M. Akram, "Palestinian Refugees and their Legal Status: Rights, politics and implications for a just solution," *Journal of Palestine Studies* 31(3) (2002) pp. 36–51.

G. W. Allport, *The Nature of Prejudice* (Cambridge, Mass.: Addison Wesley, 1954).

Joseph Alpher, Gabriel Ben-Dor, Ibrahim Dakkak, YossiI Katz, Herbert C. Kelman, Ghassan Khatib, Moshe Maoz, Nadim Rouhana, Yezid Sayyigh Zeev Schiff, Shimon Shamir and Khalil Shikaki, Concept paper: "The Palestinian Refugee Problem and the Right of Return," *Middle East Policy* 6(3) (February 1999), pp. 167–76.

Y. Amir, "Contact Hypothesis in Ethnic Relations," *Psychological Bulletin* 71 (1969), pp. 319–41.

Abd al-Salam Aql, "Palestinian Refugees of Lebanon Speak," *Journal of Palestine Studies* 25(1) (1995), pp. 54–60.

Marie Arneberg, *Living Conditions Among Palestinian Refugees Displaced in Jordan* (Oslo: Fafo draft report, 237,1997).

Nasir Aruri, and Samih Farsoun, "Palestinian Communities and Arab Host Countries," in Khalil Nakhle and Elia Zureik (eds.), *The Sociology of Palestinians* (London: Croom Helm, 1980), pp. 112–46.

Donna Arzt, *Refugees into Citizens: Palestinians and the end of the Arab–Israeli conflict* (Council on Foreign Relations Press, 1996).

Mahmood Ayoub, "Lebanon between Religious Faith and Political Ideology," in Deidre Collings (ed.), *Peace for Lebanon? From war to reconstruction* (Boulder, CO: Lynne Rienner Publishers, 1994), pp. 241–8.

Edward E. Azar, "Lebanon and its Political Culture: Conflict and integration in

Select Bibliography

Lebanon," in E. A. Azar (ed.), *The Emergence of a New Lebanon: Fantasy or reality?* (New York: Praeger Publishers, 1984).

Halim Barakat, "Social and Political Integration in Lebanon: A case of social mosaic," *The Middle East Journal* 27 (1973).

C. D. Batson, M. P. Polycarpou, E. Harmon-Jones, H. J. Imhoff, E. C. Mitchener, L. L Bednar, T. R. Klein and L. Highberger, "Empathy and Attitudes: Can feeling for a member of a stigmatized group improve feelings toward the group?," *Journal of Personality and Social Psychology* 72 (1997), pp. 105–18.

J. W. Berry and R. Kalin, "Multicultural and Ethnic attitudes in Canada: An overview of the 1991 National Survey," *Canadian Journal of Behavioral Science* 27 (1995):, pp. 301–20.

Ann Bettancourt, and Nancy Dorr, "Cooperative Interaction and Intergroup Bias: Effects of numerical representation and crosscut role assignment," *Personality and Social Psychology Bulletin* 24(12) (1998), pp. 1276–98.

E. S. Bogardus, "Measuring Social Distance," *Journal of Applied Sociology* 9 (1925), pp. 299–308.

E. S. Bogardus, *A Forty-Year Racial Distance Study* (Pasadena: University of Southern California Press, 1967).

G. J. Borjas, *Heaven's Door: Immigration policy and the American economy* (Princeton, NJ: Princeton University Press, 1999).

Fares Boueiz, "An Interview with Lebanon's Foreign Minister," *Journal of Palestine Studies* 24(1) (1994), pp. 130–2.

Nicole Brackman, "Palestinian Refugees in Lebanon: New source of cross-border tension," *The Washington Institute's Peace Watch*, 263, (May 30, 2000).

Laurie Brand, "Palestinians in Syria: The politics of integration," *The Middle East Journal* 42(4) (Autumn 1988), pp. 621–38.

Paul Brenan, *The Conflict in Northern Ireland* (Paris, Longman, 1995).

Rex Brynen, "Imagining a Solution: Final status arrangements and Palestinian refugees in Lebanon," *Journal of Palestine Studies* 26(2) (Winter 1997), pp. 42–59.

Rex Brynen, "Palestinian Refugees and the Middle East Peace Process," paper presented for the New Hampshire International Seminar/Yale Maria Lecture in Middle Eastern Studies, University of New Hampshire, April 3, 1998.

Ayse S. Caglar, "Constraining Metaphors and the Trans-Nationalization of Spaces in Berlin," *Journal of Ethnic and Migration Studies* 27(4) (October 2001), pp. 601–14.

M. Castells, "Immigrant Workers and Class Struggles in Advanced Capitalism: The Western European experience," in R. Cohen and Z. Layton-Henry (eds.), *The Politics of Migration* (Northampton, MA: Elgar, 1997), pp. 33–61.

S. Castles, *Here for Good: Western Europe's new ethnic minorities* (London: Pluto, 1984).

S. Castles, "Migrants and Minorities in Europe: Perspectives for the 1990s: Eleven hypotheses," in J. Solomos and J. Wrench (eds.), *Racism and Migration in Western Europe* (Oxford: Berg, 1993), pp. 17–34.

Hussein Chaaban, "Palestinian Refugees in Lebanon and the Host State Regulations," www.prc.org.uk/english/refugees-lebanon.

M. Chahine, "Those Left Behind," *The Middle East*, 252 (January 1996), pp. 17–19.

Select Bibliography

Helena Cobban, *The PLO: People, power and politics* (Cambridge: Cambridge University Press, 1984).

R. Cohen and Z. Layton-Henry (eds.), *The Politics of Migration* (Northampton, MA: Elgar, 1997).

Leonard Cole, "A Palestinian Return to Nowhere," *Midstream* 47(6) (2000), pp. 9–13.

S. W. Cook, "Experimenting on Social Issues," *American Psychologist* 40(1985), pp. 452–60.

S. W. Cook, "Cooperative Interaction in Multiethnic Contexts," in N. Miller and M. B. Brewer (eds.), *Groups in Contact: The psychology of desegregation* (Orlando, FL: Academic Press, 1984), pp. 175–83.

J. Cooley, "Lebanon Hopes to Join Syrian–Israeli Peace Talks," Center for Policy Analysis on Palestine, www.palestinecenter.org/cpap/pubs/19991214ib.html.

Lewis Coser, *The Functions of Social Conflict* (New York: Free Press, 1956).

R. E. Crow, "Electoral Issues: Lebanon," in J. M. Landau, F. Ozbudun and F. Tachau (eds.), *Electoral Politics in The Middle East: Issues, voters and elites* (London: Croom Helm, 1980), pp. 153–87.

Pauline Cutting, *Children of the Siege* (London: Pan Books, 1988).

Uri Davis, "Citizenship Legislation in the Syrian Arab Republic," *Arab Studies Quarterly* 18(1) (Winter 1996), pp. 29–48.

Karl Deutsch, "Social Mobilization and Political Development," *American Political Science Review* 55 (September 1961).

J. Dovidio and V. M. Esses, "Immigrants and Immigration: Advancing the psychological perspective," *Journal of Social Issues* 57(3) (Fall 2001), pp. 375–88.

J. Duckitt, *The Social Psychology of Prejudice* (New York: Praeger, 1992).

S. Edminster, *Trapped on All Sides: The marginalization of Palestinian refugees in Lebanon* (Washington, D.C.: US Committee for Refugees, 1999).

V. M. Esses, L. M. Jackson and T. L. Armstrong, "Intergroup Competition and Attitudes Toward Immigrants and Immigration: An instrumental model of group conflict," *Journal of Social Issues* 54(4) (1998), pp. 799–24.

John Fagan, and Michael O'Neill, "A Comparison of Social-Distance Scores Among College-Student Samples," *The Journal of Social Psychology* 66(2) (1965), pp. 281–90.

T. Faist, "How to Define a Foreigner? The symbolic politics of immigration in German partisan discourse, 1978–1992," in M. Baldwin-Edwards, and M. A. Schain (eds.), *The Politics of Immigration in Western Europe* (London: Frank Cass, 1994), pp. 50–71.

T. Faist, "Immigration, Integration, and the Welfare State: Germany and USA in a comparative perspective," in R. Baubock, A. Heller and A. R. Zolberg (eds.), *The Challenge of Diversity* (Aldershot: Avebury, 1996), pp. 227–58.

Hani Faris, "The Failure of Peacemaking in Lebanon: 1975–1989," in Deidre Collings (ed.), *Peace for Lebanon? From war to reconstruction* (Boulder, CO: Lynne Rienner Publishers, 1994), pp. 18–30.

Gérard Figuie, *Le Point sur le Liban* (Beyrouth: Anthologie, 1996).

K. A. Finlay and W. G. Stephan, "Reducing Prejudice: The effects of empathy on inter-group attitudes," *Journal of Applied Social Psychology* 30(8) (August 2000), pp. 1720–36.

Select Bibliography

Robert Fisk, *Pity the Nation: Lebanon at war* (London: André Deutsch, 1989).

W. S. Ford, "Interracial Public Housing in a Border City: Another look at the contact hypothesis," *American Journal of Sociology* 78 (1973), pp. 1426–47.

Robert I. Friedman, *Zealots for Zion* (New York: Random House, 1992).

S. L. Gaertner, M. C. Rust, J. F. Dovidio, B. A. Bachman and P. A. Anastasio, "The Contact Hypothesis: The role of a common in-group identity on reducing intergroup bias among majority and minority group members," in J. L. Nye and A. M. Brower (eds.), *What's Social About Social Cognition?* (Newbury Park, CA: Sage, 1996), pp. 230–360.

D. M. George and R. A. Hoppe, "Racial Identification, Preference and Self-Concept," *Journal of Cross-Cultural Psychology* 10 (1979), pp. 85–100.

Martin Gilbert, *The Arab–Israeli Conflict* (London: Weidenfeld and Nicolson, 1992).

A. Ghossein, "Geography in the Study of the Lebanese Structure and Crisis," *Haliyyat* 25 (1982), pp. 23–45.

M. W. Giles and A. Evans, "The Power Approach to Inter-group Hostility," *Journal of Conflict Resolution* 30 (1986), pp. 469–86.

Emile Habiby "Don't Blame the Victim," *New Outlook* (September–November 1990), pp. 22–8.

Simon Haddad, "The Palestinian Predicament in Lebanon," *Middle East Quarterly* (1) (2000), pp. 29–40.

Simon Haddad, "Sectarian Attitudes as a Function of Palestinian Presence in Lebanon," *Arab Studies Quarterly* 22(3) (2000), pp. 81–100.

Simon Haddad, "Christian–Muslim Relations and Attitudes toward the Lebanese State," *Journal of Muslim Minority Affairs* 21(1) (April 2001), pp. 131–48.

N. S. Hajjaj, "Palestinian Refugees in Lebanon: Until when?" The Palestinian Diaspora and Refugee Center, Shaml (July 2000).

R. F. Hamilton, *Class and Politics in the United States* (Toronto: John Wiley and Sons, 1972).

T. Hammarberg, "The Palestinian Refugees: After five decades of betrayal – time at last?" Swedish Ministry of Foreign Affairs, Stockholm, 2000.

William Harris, *Faces of Lebanon: Sects, Wars, and Global Extensions* (Princeton: Princeton University Press, 1997).

M. Hewstone and R. Brown, *Contact and Conflict in Intergroup Encounters* (Oxford: Basil Blackwell, 1986).

C. Hirschman, P. Kasinitz and J. DeWind (Eds.), *The Handbook of International Migration: The American experience* (New York: Russell Sage Foundation, 1999).

Robert Ho, "Multiculturalism in Australia: A survey of attitudes," *Human Relations* 43(3) (1990), pp. 259–72.

Albert Hourani, *Syria and Lebanon* (London: Oxford University Press, 1954).

Michael C. Hudson, *The Precarious Republic: Political modernization in Lebanon* (New York: Random House 1968).

Michael Hudson, *Arab Politics: The search for legitimacy* (Yale: Yale University Press, 1977).

Jalal al-Husseini, "UNRWA and the Palestinian Nation-Building Process," *Journal of Palestine Studies*, 29(2) (2000), pp. 51–63.

Select Bibliography

Journal of Palestine Studies, 29(2) (2000), pp. 51–63.

Salma Husseini, *Redistribution de la Population du Liban pendant la Guerre Civile (1975–1988)*, unpublished PhD thesis, EHESS (Ecole des Hautes Etudes en Sciences Sociales), Paris, June 1992.

Paul A Jureidini and Ronald D. Mclaurin, "Lebanon after the War of 1982," in Edward Azar (ed.), *The Emergence of a New Lebanon: Fantasy or reality?* (New York: Praeger Publishers, 1984).

R. Kalin and J. W. Berry, "The Social Ecology of Ethnic Attitudes in Canada," *Canadian Journal of Behavioral Science* 14 (1982), pp. 97–109.

Malcolm Kerr, "Political Decision-Making in a Confessional Democracy," in Leonard Binder (eds.), *Politics in Lebanon* (Toronto: John Wiley & Sons, 1966).

Rashid Khalidi, "The Palestinians in Lebanon: Social repercussions of Israel's invasion," *Middle East Journal* 38(3) (Spring 1984), pp. 255–66.

Chawki Khalifa, *Lubnan Bainal Geopolitik Al-Israiili Wa Al-dimografia Al Filastiniah (Lebanon between Israel's geopolitics and Palestinian demographics)* (Beirut, 2002).

Hilal Khashan and Monte Palmer, "The Economic Basis of Civil Conflict in Lebanon: A survey analysis of Sunnite Muslims," *Journal of Arab Affairs* 1(1) (October 1981), pp. 113–33.

Hilal Khashan, "Palestinian Resettlement in Lebanon: Behind the debate," *Montreal Studies on the Contemporary Arab World* (April 1994).

Hilal Khashan, "The Despairing Palestinians," *Journal of South Asian and Middle Eastern Studies* 16(1) (Fall 1992), pp. 1–17.

Hilal Khashan, *Inside the Lebanese Confessional Mind* (Lanham: University Press of America, 1992).

Hilal Khashan, "An Intifada for Peace and Against its Process," *The Arab World Geographer* 3(3) (Fall 2000), pp. 157–8.

Hilal Khashan and Simon Haddad, "The Coupling of the Syrian–Lebanese Peace Tracks: Beirut's options," *Security Dialogue* 30(2) (July 2000), pp. 201–14.

Farid al-Khazen "Permanent Settlement of Palestinians in Lebanon: A recipe for conflict," *Journal of Refugee Studies* 10(3) (1997), pp. 275–93.

Farid al-Khazen, *The Breakdown of the State in Lebanon, 1967–1976* (London: I. B. Tauris & Co. Ltd., 2000).

Philip Kunz and Yvonne Ohenebra-Sakyi, "Social Distance: A study of changing views of young Mormons toward black individuals," *Psychological Report* 65(1) (1989), pp. 195–200

Giuseppe Labianca, Daniel Brass and Barbara Gray, "Social Networks and Perceptions of Intergroup Conflict: The role of negative relationships and third parties," *Academy of Management Journal*, 41(1) (1998), pp. 55–68.

W. E. Lambert, and D. M. Taylor, *Coping with Cultural and Racial Diversity in Urban America* (New York: Praeger, 1990).

Annie Laurent and Antoine Basbous, *Guerres Secretes au Liban* (Paris: Gallimard, 1987).

Ann Lesch, "Contrasting Reactions to the Gulf Crisis: Egypt, Syria, Jordan and the Palestinians," *Middle East Journal* (Winter 1991), pp. 30–50.

R. Levine and D. T. Campbell, *Ethnocentrism: Theories of conflict, attitudes and group behavior* (New York: Wiley, 1972).

Select Bibliography

M. MacEwen, *Tackling Racism in Europe: An examination of anti-discrimination law in practice* (Washington, D.C.: Berg. 1995).

Bruce Maddy-Weitzman, "The Inter-Arab System and The Arab-Israeli Conflict: Ripening for resolution," *Journal of International Affairs* 5(1) (2000).

Joseph Maila, "The Ta'if Accord: An evaluation," in Deidre Collings (ed.), *Peace for Lebanon? From war to reconstruction* (Boulder, CO: Lynne Rienner Publishers, 1994), pp. 31–44.

Habib Malik, *Between Damascus and Jerusalem: Lebanon and the Middle East Peace*, Policy Paper 45, The Washington Institute For Near East Policy, (Washington, 2000).

L. H. Malkki, "National Geographic: The rooting of peoples and the Territorialization of National Identity Among Scholars and Refugees," *Cultural Anthropology* 7(1) (1992), pp. 24–44.

Nur Masallah, *The Palestinian Refugee Problem: Israeli plans to resettle the Palestinian refugees 1948–1972* (Ramallah: Palestinian Diaspora and Refugee Center, Shaml, 1996).

Edmond Melhem, "Workings and Shortcomings of the Lebanese Political System," *Middle East Quarterly*, 3(1) (1996).

Khalil Nakhle, "Palestinian Intellectuals and Revolutionary Transformation," in Khalil Nakhle and Elia Zureik (eds.), *The Sociology of the Palestinians* (London: Groom Helm Ltd., 1980).

Suheil al-Natour, "The Legal Status of Palestinian Refugees in Lebanon," in Refugees in the Middle East, Nordic NGO Seminar (Oslo: Norwegian Refugee Council, March 26–27, 1993).

Suheil Al-Natour, "The Legal Status of Palestinians in Lebanon," *Journal of Refugee Studies* 10(3) (1997, pp. 360–77.

Donald Neff, "US Policy and the Palestinian Refugees," *Journal of Palestine Studies* 18(1) (Autumn 1988), pp. 96–111.

T. M. Newcomb, R. H. Turner and P. E. Converse, *Social Psychology: The study of human interaction* (New York: Holt Rinehart and Winston, 1965).

Augustus R. Norton, *Amal and The Shiites: Struggle for the Soul of Lebanon* (Austin, University of Texas Press, 1987).

Edgar O'Balance, *Civil War in Lebanon, 1975–1992* (London: Macmillan, 1998).

Douglas Palmer, "Determinants of Canadian Attitudes Toward Immigration: More than just racism?" *Canadian Journal of Behavioral Science* 28(3) (1996), pp. 180–92.

Annie Murphy Paul, "Psychology's own Peace Corps: Global ethnic conflict," *Psychology Today*, 31(4) (July–August, 1998).

Michael Payne, Jr., Charles York and John Fagan "Changes in Measured Social Distance Over Time," *Sociometry* 37(2) (1974), pp. 131–6.

Shimon Peres with Arye Naor, *The New Middle East* (New York: Henry Holt, 1993).

Julie Peteet, "Identity Crisis: Palestinians in Post-War Lebanon," *Worldwide Refugee Information*, (Washington, D.C.: US Committee for Refugees, 1999).

Julie Peteet, "From Refugees to Minority: Palestinians in Post-War Lebanon," *Middle East Repor* 26(3) (July–September 1996), pp. 27–31.

JuliePeteet, "Lebanon: Palestinian Refugees in the Post-War Period,"

Select Bibliography

http://www.en.monde-diplomatique.fr/focus/mideast/region-lebanon-refugee (December, 1999).

T. F. Pettigrew (Ed.), *The Future of Social Psychology* (New York: Springer-Verlag, 1998), pp. 13–27.

T. F. Pettigrew, and R. W. Meertens, "Subtle and Blatant Prejudice in Western Europe," *European Journal of Social Psychology* 25 (1995), pp. 57–76.

T. F. Pettigrew, "Reactions toward The New Minorities of Western Europe," *Annual Review of Sociology*, 24(1) (1998), pp. 77–104.

Elisabeth Picard, *Lebanon: A shattered country* (New York: Holmes & Meier Publishers, 1996).

A. Portes and J. Curtis, "Changing Flags: Naturalization and its determinants among Mexican Americans," *International Migration Review* 21 (1987), pp. 352–71.

L. Quillian, "Prejudice as a Response to Perceived Group Threat: Population composition and anti-immigrant and racial prejudice in Europe," *American Sociological Review* 60 (1995), pp. 586–611.

Edmond Rabath, *La Formation Historique Du Liban Politique et Constitutionel* (The Formation of Historical and Political Lebanon), (Beirut: Publications de L'Universite Libanaise 1973).

Itamar Rabinovich, *The War for Lebanon 1970–1985* (Ithaca and London: Cornell University Press: , 1989).

C. Reich and M. Purbhoo, 1975, "The Effects of Cross-Cultural Contact," *Canadian Journal of Behavioral Science* 7, pp. 313–27.

Hala Nawfal Rizkallah, *Al-Falastiniiuun fi lubnan wa suria dirasat dimougrafiat moukaranat* (The Palestinians in Lebanon and Syria: A comparative demographic study), (Beirut: Dar Al-Jadid, 1998).

Walter Rosenbaum, *Political Culture* (New York: Praeger, 1975).

Joseph Rothschild, *Ethnopolitics: A conceptual framework* (New York: Columbia University Press, 1981).

R. G. Rumbaut, N. Foner and S. J. Gold, "Transformations: Introduction. Immigration and Immigration Research in the United States," *American Behavioral Scientist* 42 (1999), pp. 1258–63.

S. A. Saade, *The Social Structure of Lebanon: Democracy or servitude?* (Beirut: Edition Dan An-Nahar, 1993).

Wadie Said, "The Palestinians in Lebanon: The rights of the victims of the Palestinian–Israeli peace process," *Columbia Human Rights Law Review* 30(2) (Spring 1999), pp. 315–57.

Nawaf Salam, "Between Repatriation and Resettlement: Palestinian refugees in Lebanon," *The Journal of Palestine Studies* 24(1) (Autumn 1994), pp. 18–28.

Elie Salem, "Lebanon's Political Maze: The search for Peace in a turbulent land," *Middle East Journal*, 33(1979), pp. 444–63.

Kamal Salibi, *Crossroads to the Civil War: Lebanon 1958–1976* (Delmar: Caravan Books, 1976).

Rosemary Sayyigh, "Palestinians in Lebanon: Status ambiguity, insecurity and flux," *Race and Class* 30(1) (July–September 1988), pp. 13–32.

Rosemary Sayyigh, "Palestinians in Lebanon: Pawns on a tilted chessboard," www.between-lines.org/archives (June 2001).

Select Bibliography

Rosemary Sayigh "The Palestinians in Lebanon: A painful present and uncertain future," *Majallat al-Dirasat al-Filastiniyya*, 13 (Winter 1993).

Rosemary Sayyigh, "Palestinians in Lebanon: Uncertain future," in Deirdre Collings (ed.), *Peace For Lebanon? From war to reconstruction* (London: Lynne Rienner Publishers, 1994).

Rosemary Sayyigh, "Palestinians in Lebanon: Harsh present, uncertain future," *Journal of Palestine Studies* 25(1) (Autumn 1995), pp. 37–53.

Rosemary Sayyigh, "Dis/Solving the Refugee Problem," *Middle East Report*, 207 (Summer 1998).

Rosemary Sayyigh, *Too Many Enemies: The Palestinian experience in Lebanon* (London and New Jersey: Zed Books Ltd, 1994).

Rosemary Sayyigh, "Palestinian Refugees in Lebanon: Implantation, transfer or return?" *Middle East Policy* 7(1) (2001), pp. 95–105.

Rosemary Sayyigh, "No Work, No Space, No Future: Palestinian refugees in Lebanon," *Middle East International*, August 10, 2001.

Brenda Seaver, "The Regional Sources of Power Sharing Failure: The case of Lebanon," *Political Science Quarterly* 115(2) (2001), pp. 247–73.

Selah Selah, "Les Refugies Palestiniens au Liban," *Revue d'Etudes Palestiniennes*, 23 (Printemps, 2000).

Abbas Shiblak, "Residency Status and Civil Rights of Palestinians in Host Arab States", *Journal of Palestine Studies* 25(3) (1996), pp. 36–45.

Issam Sleiman, "Equilibre Confessionnel et Equilibre Institutionnel au Liban", in *Le Liban D'aujourd'hui,* F. Kiwan (ed.) (Paris: Cermoccurs Editions, 1994).

Reuben Slonim, "Palestinian Refugee Camps Breed Future Threat to Israel," *Journal of Palestine Studies* 12(2) (1983), pp. 194–6.

Peter Sluglett and Marion Farouk Sluglett, *The Times Guide to the Middle East* (London: Times Books, 1991).

Arnon Soffer, "Lebanon – Where Demography Is the Core of Politics and Life," *Middle Eastern Studies* 22 (1986), pp. 197–205.

F. Solomos, and J. Wrench, "Race and Racism in Contemporary Europe," in J. Solomos and J. Wrench (eds.), *Racism and Migration in Western Europe* (Oxford: Berg, 1993), pp. 3–16.

Stephen J. Sosebee, "Progress toward Statehood Tightens Noose around Palestinians in Lebanon," *Washington Report on Middle East Affairs* (February/March 1996).

W. G. Stephan, O. Ybbara, C. Martinez, J. Schwarzwald and M. Tur-Kaspa, "Prejudice toward Immigrants to Spain and Israel: An integrated threat theory analysis," *Journal of Cross-Cultural Psychology* 29 (1998), pp. 559–76.

W. G. Stephan and Krystina Finlay, "The role of empathy in improving inter-group relations," *Journal of Social Issues* 55(4) (Winter 1999).

Jaber Suleiman, "The Current Political Organizational, and Security Situation in the Palestinian Refugee Camps of Lebanon," *Journal of Palestine Studies* 29(1) (Autumn 1999), pp. 66–75.

W. G. Sumner, *Folkways* (New York: Ginn, 1906).

Mohammed Tahri and Maria Donato, "Refugees also have Rights: Palestinian refugees in Lebanon and Jordan", EMHRN Mission Report, published by the Euro-Mediterranean Human Rights Network, (September 17–18, 2000).

Select Bibliography

Mark Tessler, and Jody Nachtwey, "Palestinian Political Attitudes: An analysis of survey data from the West Bank and Gaza", *Israel Studies* 4(1) (1999), pp. 22–43.

Sybilla G. Thicknesse, *Arab Refugees: A Survey of Resettlement Possibilities* (London: Royal Institute for International Affairs, 1949).

N. Tienhaara, *Canadian Views on Immigration and Population* (Ottawa: Information Canada, 1974).

Stephen Tuch, Lee Sigleman and Jason Macdonald, "The Polls – Trends: Race relations and American youth, 1976–1995," *Public Opinion Quarterly* 63(11) (1999), pp. 109–14.

Hanser Verlag, "Hansers Sozialgeschichte der Deutschen Literatur," vom 16 *Jahrhundert bis zur Gegenwart* 12, (1996).

Sabine Von Dirke, "Multikulti: The German debate on multiculturalism," *German Studies Review* 17(3) (1994), pp. 513–36.

Said Wadie, "The Palestinians in Lebanon: The rights of the victims of the Palestinian–Israeli peace process," *Columbia Human Rights Law Review* 30(2) (Spring 1999), pp. 31–57.

Sigrid Weigel, "Literature der Fremde – Literature in der Fremde," in Klaus Briegleb and Sigrid Weigel (eds.), *Gegenwartsliteratur seit 1968* (München and Wien: Carl).

Morton Weinfeld, "The Social Integration of Immigrants and the Response of Institutions," draft paper, Miami: Trans-Atlantic Learning Community, Migration Group (Toronto: McGill University, Department of Sociology, April 1, 1998).

Charles Westin, "The Effectiveness of Settlement and Integration Policies Toward Immigrants and Their Descendants in Sweden," Geneva: Migration Branch, International Labor Office, *International Migration Papers* 34 (2001).

R. M. Williams, *Strangers Next Door: Ethnic relations in American communities* (Englewood Cliffs, NJ: Prentice-Hall, 1964).

C. Wilpert, "Ideological and Institutional Foundations of Racism in the Federal Republic of Germany", in Solomos and Wrench (eds.), *Racism and Migration in Western Europe* (Oxford: Berg, 1993), pp. 67–81.

Charles Winslow, *Lebanon: War and politics in a fragmented society* (London and New York: Routledge, 1996).

Philip Q. Yang, "Explaining Immigrant Naturalization," *International Migration Review* 28(3) (Fall 1994), pp. 449–78.

R. B. Zajonc, "Attitudinal Effects of Mere Exposure," *Journal of Personality and Social Psychology* Monograph 9 (2, Part 2) (1968), pp. 1–28.

S. Ziegler, "Measuring Inter-Ethnic Attitudes in a Multi-Ethnic Context," *Canadian Ethnic Studies* 12 (1980), pp. 45–55.

M. Zuaytir, *Al-Mashruu al-Maruni fi Lubnan* (The Maronite Project in Lebanon), (Beirut: Wikalat al-Tawzii al-Duwaliyya).

Index

Abbassieh outpost (Israeli Army), 140
Abul-Aynayn, Brigadier Sultan, 138
accommodation, 40
   see also integration
Acre (Israel), 23
Adelson, Leslie, 67
Ain al-Hilweh (Palestinian camp,
   Lebanon), 34, 35, 79, 80n, 93, 97, 115
Al-Amin, Abdullah, 2
Al-Bass (Palestinian camp, Lebanon), 34
Al-Khazen, Farid, 32, 82
Al-Qaeda terror network, 80n
Albright, Madeleine, 17
Aleppo (Syria), 24
alienation, 123
Allport, G. W., 92
Amal militia, 34, 84, 88, 129
Amin, Abdullah, 35
ANOVA/Analysis of Variance Test, 79
anti-Palestinianism, 47, 84, 96–7, 142
Aoun, General Michel, 15
Arab intellectuals, 134
Arab Liberation Front, 38n
Arab Peace Initiative, 134
Arab Socialist Ba'ath Party (Syria), 26
Arab world, 26, 134
   inter-Arab fragmentation, 36
   Maronite absorption into, 6
   as refugee hosts, 40, 143
   tolerance of Palestinians, 138
   unification of, 26
Arab–Israeli borders, 108
Arab–Israeli conflict, 1, 8, 15, 30
   and refugee problem, 22
   see also Israeli–Palestinian talks
Arab–Israeli negotiations, 112–13, 128, 138,
   143, 146
Arabism, 26
Arafat, Yasser, 34, 114, 128–30, 136
Arida, Antun (Maronite Patriarch), 29
Aridi, Ghazi, 46
Armenia, 110
   Armenian immigration to Lebanon, 93,
   124–5

Asad, President Bashar, 17, 21n
Aussiedler (foreigners), 66–7
Australia, multiculturalism in, 71, 122–3
Azerbaijan, 110

Baddawi (Palestinian camp, Lebanon), 34
Barak, Prime Minister Ehud, 20, 105, 143
Barid River (Lebanon), 23
Beirut Arab Summit (2002), 134
Beirut (Lebanon), 2, 16, 20
   Amal attacks in, 129
   Armenian immigrants to, 93
   camps in, 34
   capture by Israeli forces of, 33
   Christian–Palestinian violence in, 86
   as commercial center, 23
   rejection of permanent Palestinian settle-
      ment, 44
Bekaa Valley (Lebanon), 23, 33
   concentration of Palestinians in, 93
   Fatah conflict in, 34
Ben-Gurion, Prime Minister David, 26
Berry, J. W., 70
"Black September," 27
Boueiz, Fares, 35, 46, 115
Bourj al-Barajneh (Palestinian camp,
   Lebanon), 34, 93, 97
Bourj al-Shamali (Palestinian camp,
   Lebanon), 34
Brenan, Paul, 96
Britain *see* United Kingdom

Cairo Agreement (1969), 31
Cairo (Egypt), 30, 35
camps
   armed Palestinians in, 107–8
   camp-dwellers, 43
   clashes in, 97
   exodus from, 33
   frustration in, 128
   as hotbeds of radicalism, 80
   inhabitants of, 88
   military presence in, 145
   Palestinian and Shi'ite residence near, 93

171

Index

political presence in, 129
see also Ain al-Hilweh; al-Bass; Baddawi; Bourj al-Barajneh; Bourj al-Shamali; Mar Elias; Mieh Mieh; Nahr al-Barid; Rashidieh; Sabra; Shatila; War of the Camps
Canada, 2, 143
  attitudes toward immigration, 69–70
  housing project plan, 143
  inter-group relations in, 98
  offer to absorb Palestinians, 115, 138
  support for Palestinian settlement, 112
"carte de sejour" (French visa), 115
castes, 5
Castles, S., 66
Catholics, 125
  see also Greek-Catholics
census (1932), 7, 32
Chamoun, Dory, 108, 109
change, and ethnic conflict, 125
Chehab, President Fouad, 41
Chirot, Daniel, 125
Chouf mountains (Lebanon), 112, 115
Christian democratic heartland project, 7
Christian right, the, 86, 110
Christians, 3, 5, 31, 47
  alienation of, 111
  attitude toward Armenians, 125
  attitude toward Palestinians, 82, 84–6, 100–2, 110, 142, 145
  fear of permanent Palestinian presence, 107
  and Muslims, 6–8, 94, 95
  and Palestinian rights, 114
  President of Lebanon, 9
  view of intermarriage, 99
  see also Greek-Catholics; Greek-Orthodox; Maronites
citizens, 2
  obligations of, 68
citizenship, acquisition of, 66, 68, 115
civil marriages, 93, 95
  introduction of, 99
civil rights *see* rights, civil
civil war *see* Lebanese civil war
Clinton, President Bill, 16
communal groups, 75
  armed action and, 109
  closeness and hostility, 89n
  communal contract, 111
  differences, 86
  inter-communal bonds, 3, 124, 142
  see also inter-group relations
communication, relationship with positive view, 122
communication theory, 123–4
community, sense of, 124

compensation, 147n
"Conference on the Palestinians in Advanced Lebanon," 117n
confessional democracy, 5, 29, 47
confessional homogeneity, 95
conflict
  ethnic, 125
  low-level, 133
  nature of, 122
constitution, 2, 143
contact, with Palestinians, 92
contact hypothesis, 69–70
Cook, S. W., 98
Coser, Lewis, 124
Council of Maronite Bishops, 21n
cultural enclaves, 68
  dissimilarity of, 124
culture
  acquisition of, 67
  dominant, 98

Dallul, Muhsin, 35
Damascus (Syria), 15, 16, 24
  relationship with Hizbullah, 17
Democratic Front for the Liberation of Palestine (DFLP), 34, 140n
  see also Palestinian Authority; Palestinian Liberation Organization; Popular Front of the Liberation of Palestine
democratic political systems, 110
demographic balance/composition, 1, 3–5, 46, 110
  lack of majority, 111
  legislative safeguards for, 145
  see also Muslim–Christian demographic balance
deportation, 115
Deutch, Karl, 124
diaspora (Palestinian), 22, 114, 146
difference, cultural, 67
Dinnieh (Islamic Palestinian group), 79
Directorate for Palestinian Refugee Affairs, 4
discrimination
  boundaries of, 7, 66, 97
  direct and indirect, 66
displacement, 40
  see also Palestinian displacement
Document of National Understanding *see* Ta'if Accord
Druze, 5, 47, 77
  interaction with Christians, 95
  opposition to naturalization, 104
  Palestinian settlement and, 141
  Palestinians and, 85, 87, 93, 114
  political position of, 112

Index

Druze–Sunni interests, 115

East Jerusalem *see* Jerusalem
Economic Survey Mission reports, 25
economy
  agricultural, 23
  post-civil war, 106, 144
Edde, Michel, 2, 46
Egypt, 26
  as champions of Palestinian cause, 134
  see also Nasser, Gamal Abdel
El-Khazen, Farid Elias, 141
El-Khuri, President Bishara, 29
elections, 104–5
emigration, 45
empathy, 75, 87–8, 122
  cross-group, 98
equal opportunities, lack of, 125
equal representation, 111
ethnic density, 70
ethnic groups, competition between, 125
ethnic warfare, 110
ethnocentrism, 71, 123
ethnocentrism scale, 71
Europe *see* France; Germany; United Kingdom
exile, 131

Fafo Institute for Applied Social Science, 140n
Fakhuri, Shawqi, 35
Farhat, Brigadier General Nabih, 35
Fatah (Victory Movement), 30, 128, 130, 134
  control of southern Lebanon camps by, 34
  split within, 33, 129
fedayeen (Arab commandos), 31
"final status" negotiations, 20, 143
Finlay, K. A., 88
firepower, as source of political expression, 85
foreign plots, 1, 113
France, 7, 65, 115, 146
friendship, importance of, 98

Galilee (Israel), 83
Gastarbeiter (guest workers), 66
Gaza Strip, 25, 114, 131
  hopes for Palestinian state in, 131
Gemayel, Pierre, 89
Gemayel, President Amin, 16
Gemayel, President Bashir, assassination of, 33
General Bureau of Palestinian Affairs (Lebanon), 41
George, D. M., 70

Germany, 65
  refugee integration in, 66–8
  Turks in, 67
"ghetto," 115
  notion of, 68
Ghossein, A., 6
Golan Heights, 18
"Grapes of Wrath" operation, 17
Greater Lebanon, 6
Greek-Catholics, 5
  and Palestinians, 93
  in Lebanon, 77
Greek-Orthodox, 5
  and Palestinians, 93
  in Lebanon, 77
"green card" (US visa), 115
group hostility, 91
guerillas *see* Palestinian guerillas
Gulf States, 36, 113, 134
Gulf War (1991), 36, 138

Habash, George, 38n
Haddad, Major Saad, 33
  see also Lebanese Army
Haifa (Israel), 23
Hamas, 81n, 129
  see also Hizbullah; Islamic Jihad
"Haraka al-Mahroumin" political movement, 34
Hariri, Prime Minister Rafik, 16, 41, 115
  on Palestinian integration, 143
  on peace with Israel, 20n
Hasbani River (Lebanon), 19
hegemony, regional, 19
Helou, President Charles, 30
hierarchical inclusion procedure, 120
Hizbullah, 17, 18, 79, 84, 114, 129
  tactics of, 136–7
  and War of the Camps, 88–9
  see also Hassan Nasrallah
Ho, Robert, 71, 123
Hoppe, R. A., 70
Hoss, Prime Minister Salim, 19, 45
Hourani, Albert, 5
Hout, Shafiq, 108
Hrawi, President Elias, 95, 105
humanitarianism, 24–5
Hussein, Saddam, 36

identity, Lebanese, 9n
  collective, 124
  national, 69
  see also nationalism, Arab
Iklim al-Tufah (Lebanon), 84
immigration, 65–6
  benefits of, 68
  moral aspect of, 67

Index

imperialism, 26
implantation *see* tawtin
income levels, 79
independence of Lebanon, 6
indifference, 47
integration, 2–3, 22, 100, 126
   functional, 96
   integrated housing, 97
   Palestinian, 40–4
   socio-economic, 25, 42, 91–102, 115
   see also accommodation
inter-communal ties *see* communal groups, inter-communal bonds
inter-group relations, 41, 71, 75, 92, 98, 116, 118, 119, 122
   competition between, 69
   in-group/out-group relations, 124
interaction, 94
Interior Ministry, 4
intermarriage, 44
internal migration, 92
Intifada (1987), 134
Intifada (second, 2000), 18, 134, 135, 145
intimate relations, 99
intra-Palestinian conflict, 34
Iraq
   American assault against, 139
   Ba'ath Party, 38n
   PLO support for, 36
Iraq Petroleum Company, 23
irrigated lands, 23
Islamic fundamentalists *see* Dinnieh; Hamas; Hizbullah; Islamic Jihad
Islamic Jihad, 18, 129
Islamization of Lebanon, 84
Israel *see* State of Israel
Israeli Army, 33
Israeli invasion (1982), 5
Israeli–Palestinian talks, 108, 146

Jabril, Ahmed, 38n
Jaffa (Israel), 23
Jamat al-Nur, 81n
Jerusalem, 129, 131
Jordan, 27, 29
   concern with Palestinian refugees, 37
   Palestinians in, 40
   treaty with Israel and, 133
Jordan Valley, 25
Jumblatt, Kamal, 87
Jumblatt, Walid, 115, 143
Jureidini, Paul, 29
just peace, likelihood of, 133–4

Kalin, R., 70
Karam, Simon, 19
Karameh, battle of, 134

Karami, Ahmed, 2
Kataeb Party (Lebanon), 32, 86
Khalifa, Colonel Chawki, 116n
Khalil, Abu, 89
Khashan, Hilal, 115, 132
King Abdullah (Jordan), 113
King Hussein (Jordan), 27, 31
Kissinger, Henry, 89
Kuwait, reprisals against Palestinians, 36

labor dilemma, 101
labor law, 130
labor market, 100–1
Lahoud, President Emile, 2, 45, 108, 144, 145
Lake Yamuna *see* Bekaa Valley
Lausanne conference (1949), 23, 25
Leadership of Palestinian National Action in Lebanon, 35
Lebanese Army, 31, 35, 79
Lebanese authorities, 100, 139
   position on camps, 107–8
   public familiarity with, 110
   use of Lebanese territory, 146
Lebanese civil war (1975–90), 1, 5, 8, 15, 32, 110
   displacement caused by, 43
   legacy of, 91, 122, 124
   memories of, 46, 141
   Palestinian blame for, 82
   power vacuum created by, 85
   proposed resumption of, 103, 106, 107–8
Lebanese Forces
   defeat in Mountain War, 87
   slaughter in Palestinian camps by, 33
Lebanese government
   attitude toward refugees, 130
   Christian citizenship grants, 104
   lack of confidence in, 95
   official policy of, 114
Lebanese media, 2, 112, 114
Lebanese nation, concept of, 44, 124
Lebanese public, 142
Lebanese–Israeli border, 30, 31
Lebanese–Palestinian dialogue, 35
Lebanese–Palestinian relations, 29
Lebanese–Syrian relationship, 16, 19
Lebanon *see* Beirut; demographic composition; Maronites; Palestinian refugees; permanent settlement; resettlement; Shi'ites; Sunnis; Ta'if Accord
Litani operation, 33
Litani River (Lebanon), 23

McLaurin, Ronald, 29
Madrid, 1, 19, 143
Madrid Peace Conference, 36

Index

Maila, Joseph, 107, 145
Makassed (Sunni cultural institution), 42
Malik, Habib, 145
Mar Elias (Palestinian camp, Lebanon), 34
marginalization, 124
Maronite League, 103, 105
  see also Christians; Maronites
Maronites, 9, 77
  domination by, 8, 11n, 31
  fear of Muslims, 32, 84
  misfortunes of, 111
  and Palestinians, 93
  perspective on civil war, 86
  political dominance, 114
  social and historical boundaries of, 6
  see also Christians
May 17, 1983 Agreement, 16
media (Lebanese), 2
mere exposure hypothesis, 69–70
Middle East *see* Egypt; Iraq; Jordan; Palestine; State of Israel; Syria
Mieh Mieh (Palestinian camp, Lebanon), 34
militia power, 85
Ministry of Labor (Lebanon), 42
minorities, indigenous view of, 66
Moghaizel, Fadi, 101
Morris, Benny, 22
Mountain War (1983) *see* War of the Mountains
multi-confessional state, 3
multiculturalism, 70, 122–3
  in Australia, 71
Munir Maqdah, 134
Murr, Michael, 105
Musa, Abu, 33
Muslim–Christian cooperation, 95
Muslim–Christian demographic balance, 5, 8–9, 32
Muslims, 3, 5, 30, 47
  activism among, 31
  attempts to increase political representation by, 32
  and Christians, 6–8, 94
  conflict with Israel, 110
  growing discontent among, 47
  opposition to, 31
  sympathy toward Palestinians, 88, 101, 146
  see also Palestinian Muslims; Shi'ites; Sunnis

Nahr al-Barid (Palestinian camp, Lebanon), 34
Nasrallah, Hassan, 45, 114
  see also Hizbullah
Nasser, Gamal Abdel, 26

The National Block, 38n
National Liberal Party (Lebanon), 38n, 108
The National Pact, 7–8
National Salvation Front (NSF), 34
nationalism
  Arab, 8, 11n, 26, 30, 141
  Palestinian, 134
Native Indians, 70
naturalization, 41, 103
  Arab prohibition of, 40
  mass, 106
naturalization decree, 103–4, 105, 145
negativism, 47
North African states, 134
Northern Ireland, 96, 125
Norton, Augustus R., 142

Occupied Territories, 20, 34
  liberation of, 108
  see also Gaza Strip; West Bank
"Operation Peace for Galiliee," 33
Osbat al-Ansar *see* Hamas
Oslo Accords (1993), 2, 36–7, 129, 133–4
"otherness," 40

PA *see* Palestinian Authority
Palestine, 22, 26, 45, 134, 137–8, 145
  exodus from, 46
  see also Palestinian refugees
Palestine Conciliation Commission, 24
Palestinian Authority, 107, 113–14, 145
  negotiations with Israel, 143
  as voice of Palestinian people, 128
Palestinian camps, 3
  cleansing of, 122
Palestinian cause, 88
Palestinian Christians, 142
Palestinian community, size of, 4
Palestinian data sample, 79–80
Palestinian displacement, 83
Palestinian guerillas, 86, 106
  eviction from Jordan, 27
  threat of, 136
Palestinian homeland, 30
  see also Palestine
Palestinian Liberation Organization (PLO), 31, 134
  alienation of Gulf States, 36
  challenge to, 34
  control of Ain al-Hilweh camp, 79
  decline of, 128–30
  defeat of in Lebanon, 35
  eviction from Israel, 87
  lack of funding from, 101
  military presence in Lebanon, 84
  moderate stance of, 37–8n
  relocation of power base to Lebanon, 27

175

Index

as Sunni Muslim army, 84
two-state solution and, 132
Palestinian militarism, 84
Palestinian Muslims, 32
Palestinian refugees, 1
  allegiance of, 128
  and Arab nationalist cause, 26, 141
  background to crisis, 22
  blame for war, 86
  citizenship issue, 115
  demand for civil and social rights, 35
  deportation of, 1
  Druze and, 85
  education and, 42–3
  ethnic composition of, 32
  existence in post-war Lebanon, 131, 145
  expulsion from Christian-controlled areas, 92
  fate of in Arab world, 37
  influx of, 30
  and Lebanese demographic balance, 110
  Lebanese perceptions of, 43–4, 118–26
  as Lebanon's twentieth sect, 9
  legal and socio-political standing of, 2
  levels of hostility and empathy toward, 82–9
  Muslim character of, 142
  narrative of, 27n, 115
  naturalization of, 41
  negative stereotypes of, 43–4
  number of, 4
  opposition to, 19
  permanent residence of, 1
  permanent settlement of, 19, 46, 106–7, 109, 137–9
  plight of, 80, 91, 128: during Cold War, 27
  politics of, 88
  reintegration into exclusive spaces, 122
  relationship with SES levels, 123
  relief work with, 24
  residence in Lebanon, 93
  rights of, 29, 100–2, 114
  as security issue, 132
  socio-economic exclusion of, 130
  status of, 2
  and Sunni Lebanese, 82–3
  as "sword" of the Sunnis, 84
  targets for violence, 88
  threat to State of Israel, 116–17
  as "time bomb," 2, 105
  tolerance of, 96–101
  treated as foreigners, 42
  underclass resentment of, 142
  as victims of discrimination, 41
  visas for, 42
  welfare policy, 100

Palestinian refugee camps see Ain al-Hilweh; al-Bass; Baddawi; Bourj al-Barajneh;Bourj al-Shamali; Mar Elias; Mieh Mieh; Nahr al-Barid; Rashidieh; Sabra; Shatila; War of the Camps
Palestinian rejectionists, 38n, 107, 136
Palestinian resettlement, 44–7
Palestinian–Lebanese relationship, 142
Palestinian-ness, 134
Palestinian–Shi'ite rivalry, 84
Palestinian–Sunni affinity, 142
Palestinization of Lebanon, 111
Palmer, Monte, 142
parallel empathy, 88
Party of God see Hizbullah
peace, just peace, 133–4
peace coalition, 133
peace process, 2, 137
  collapse of, 131, 139
  impact of, 132
"peoplehood," 40
Peres, Prime Minister Shimon, 144
permanent settlement, 1, 19, 46, 106–7
  opposition to, 141, 144
  popular attitudes toward, 75
  steps toward, 41
  Sunni views on, 45
  threat to Lebanese regime, 145
permanent status negotiations, 113–14
Peteet, Julie, 43, 97
Phalange Party see Kataeb Party
PLO see Palestinian Liberation Organization
pluralism, 95, 123
political equation, the, 125
political rights see rights, political
Popular Front for the Liberation of Palestine (PFLP), 34, 134
  see also Democratic Front for the Liberation of Palestine
population, rural and urban, 23
power-sharing, 6, 111, 125
pro-Palestinian voices, 143
propaganda war, 36
Protestants, 125
  see also Christians; Maronites
Public Works Ministry (Lebanon), 23
Purbhoo, M., 70, 98

Qaddumi, Farouk, 35
Qana (Lebanon), 17
quality of study data, 77–9
Quillan, L., 69
Qurai, 115

radicalism, support for, 135–7

Index

Radio Cairo, 26
Rashidieh (Palestinian camp, Lebanon), 34
reactive empathy, 88
reconstruction phase, 141
refugee camps *see* camps
Refugee Working Group, 20, 36, 143
refugees *see* Palestinian refugees
regional instability, 133
Reich, C., 70, 98
relationships, direct linear, 70
"relief works," 25
religion, 92–3
   influence of, 121
   religious dissent, 99
religious communities, 5–6
   size of, 3
repatriation, 22, 139, 141
resettlement, 3, 22, 96
   attitudes toward, 118–25
   domestic implications of, 103
   economic fears over, 107
   economic repercussions of, 106
   expected political impact of, 110–12
   imposed settlement, 103, 108–9, 112–16
   indirect resettlement, 146–7
   Lebanese agreement on, 141
   Lebanese public opposition to, 106
   permanent settlement outside Palestine, 137–9
   potential for communal conflict and, 145
   schemes and suggestions, 23–4
   studies on, 2
   see also permanent settlement
revolutionary consciousness, 98
right of return, 22, 114, 137, 138
   abandonment of, 139
   legal and moral claims of, 143
   narrative interpretations of, 115–16
   negation of, 45
rights
   civil, 1, 41, 100–2, 146
   natural, 22
   political, 25, 68
   social and economic, 114
   see also right of return
Rosenbaum, Walter, 124
Rothschild, Joseph, 123–4

Sabra (Palestinian camp, Lebanon), 33, 34, 88
Sadr, Imam Musa, 34
Salah, Salah, 35
Salameh, Ghassan, 19
Salibi, Kamal, 7
Saudi Arabia, 15, 36
Sayyigh, Rosemary, 42, 44, 97, 141

schools, 97
   Lebanese, 98
second Intifada *see* Intifada (second, 2000)
sectarian balance, 106, 116
sectarianism, 4, 6, 7, 9, 94, 130, 145
sects, relationship between, 124
sedentarism, 68
segregation, 96
   housing, 43, 97
SES *see* socio-economic status
settlement *see* resettlement
Sfeir, Cardinal Nasrallah, 46, 103, 144
Sharon, Prime Minister Ariel, 132
Shatila (Palestinian camp, Lebanon), 33, 34, 88, 93, 97, 129
Shebaa Farms (Lebanon), 18, 21n
Shi'ites, 5, 34, 47, 77
   assertion of power, 87
   attitude toward Armenians, 125
   Israeli retaliation against, 84
   opposition to naturalization, 104
   and Palestinians: attitude toward, 82, 114, 142, 145; interaction with, 123
   political tensions amongst, 94
   Speaker of Parliament, 9
   see also Amal militia
Shururu, Fadl, 35
Sidon (Lebanon), 35, 79
Sinai, 25
Six Day War (1967), 30, 134
   Arab defeat in, 27
Sixth Brigade of the Lebanese Army, 34
skepticism, Palestinian, 132
Slonim, Reuben, 134
social change movement, 31
Social Distance Scale, 126n
socio-economic status (SES), 121, 123
socio-economic ties, 44
solidarity, cultural, 67
Solomos, J., 65
sources of study data, 76–7
South Lebanon Army *see* Lebanese Army; Haddad, Major Saad
Southern Mount Lebanon (Shuff and Aley region), 94
Soviet Union
   interest in Middle East, 26
   as patron of radical Arab regimes, 36
spiritual leaders conference (September 1999), 109
stability
   promotion of, 7
   see also solidarity, cultural
State of Israel, 15
   absorption of refugees into, 25
   Ben-Gurion government, 25, 26
   creation of, 24, 29, 115

Index

cross-border attacks against, 86, 135
defense system surrounding, 33
eviction of PLO from (1982), 87
invasion of Lebanon (1982), 86, 134
and Jerusalem, 129
Jewish character of, 144
Lebanese negotiations with, 16–17
Palestinian negotiations with, 36–7, 108
pre-emptive raids by, 33
refugee narrative in, 115
relations with Arab world and, 133–4
and right of return, 143–4
security and, 30, 133
talks with Syria, 20
"state within a state" concept, 31, 32
statehood, desire for, 134
statistical analysis tools
  avoidance mechanism, 96
  regression equation, 121, 123
  stepwise regression, 119, 120
Stephan, W. G., 69, 88
Sumner, W. G., 71
Sunnis, 5, 31, 47, 77
  attitude toward Armenians, 125
  exclusion from Tripartite Agreement (1985), 87
  mobilization of, 87
  opposition to naturalization, 104
  political demands of, 141
  Prime Minister, 9
  resettlement and, 114, 141
  solidarity with Palestinians, 82–3, 94
superpower bipolarity, 26
"Surete Generale" (State Security Service), 4, 41
survey instrument, 76
Syria, 5
  absorption of refugees into, 23
  anger at Lebanon during 1967 war, 30
  Ba'ath Party, 38n
  concern with Palestinian refugees, 37
  dilemma of labor workers in, 101
  industry in, 24
  and Israel, 20, 133
  military and political disadvantage, 15
  negotiating strategy, 17–18
  Palestinians in, 40
  subservience of Lebanon to, 15–16, 19, 145
  support of rebel Fatah movement, 33–4

Ta'if, 15
Ta'if Accord (1989), 8, 15, 35, 94, 111, 141
  post-Ta'if Lebanon, 9, 95
  and security effect in Lebanon, 109–10
Tal al-Zaatar, slaughter at, 88
tawtin, 46, 141
Tel Aviv, 17

terrorism, 133
"The Civil and Social Rights of the Palestinian People," 35–6
Tienhara, N., 69
tolerance, 96
tolerance scale, 123
traditional values, 66
Treaty of Brotherhood, Cooperation and Coordination (1991), 16
Tripartite Agreement (1985), 87
Tripoli (Libya), 23, 34
Turkey *see* Beirut, Armenian immigrants to; Germany, Turks in
two-state solution, 132

UN demarcation line (1949), 19
UN Resolution 425, 16, 17
UN Resolution 194 (III), 24, 26
unemployment, 46, 130
United Kingdom, 65
United Nations Interim Force in Lebanon (UNIFIL), 33
United Nations Refugee Rehabilitation Fund, 25
United Nations Relief and Works Agency (UNRWA), 4, 24, 27, 101
  provisions for Palestinians, 43
United Nations Security Council, 16
United States, 146
  black–white interracial contact in, 66
  immigration to, 68–9, 115
  as Middle East intermediary, 133
  pressure on Israel of, 25
  racial intolerance in, 70
  role of, 16–17
  support for Palestinian settlement, 112–13, 117n
University of Washington, 125
upper class, resurgence of, 111
USSR *see* Soviet Union

variables, 75–6

War of the Camps (1987), 2, 5, 33–4, 84, 88
War of the Mountains (1983), 83, 94
Washington, D.C. (US), 15
Wazzani Springs (Lebanon), 19
wealth, 45–6
West
  emigration to, 115
see also France; Germany; United Kingdom; United States
West Bank, 27, 114, 131
  hopes for Palestinian state in, 132
Wilpert, C., 66
work permits, issue of, 42, 131
working class, imported, 42
World War I, 93

178

Index

Wrench, J., 65
xenophobia, 123
Yugoslavia, 110

Zahlé (Lebanon), 104
Ziegler, S., 70
Zionism/Zionists, 22, 26